Financially SECURE Forever

"Understanding why we do what we do with our money based on the science of how the brain works will lead to better, less stressful decision making over time. The ability to plan, delay gratification and eventually reach your financial goals is locked inside the wiring of this ever evolving tool we call our brain. This book helps unlock the pathway to making the right financial decisions in today's world."

DANIEL R. MASIELLO,
CFP®, CLU®, ChFC®, CFS®, LUTCF®

Financially
SECURE
Forever

The Seasons of Advice® Solution

**NEUROECONOMIC-BASED STRATEGIES
FOR MAKING SOUND FINANCIAL DECISIONS**

Charles Hamowy, CPA, CFP® | Christopher Conigliaro, CFP®

Foreword by Harvard Neuroscientist Srini Pillay, MD

Published by HCA Consulting, Inc.
1370 Avenue of the Americas
New York, NY 10019
www.Financially-Secure-Forever.com

Library of Congress Cataloguing-in-Publication Data

Charles Hamowy, CPA, CFP and Christopher Conigliaro, CFP

Financially SECURE Forever
The Seasons of Advice® Solution

Published by HCA Consulting
ISBN 978-0-615-79617-8

1. Personal Finance 2. Wealth Management 3. Business & Investing
4. Budgeting & Money Management, 5. Retirement Planning

Edited by Judy Katz, Katz Creative, Inc.
Art Direction by Wendy Glavin
Cover and Book design by Rebecca Saraceno, Rebeccaink
Proofreading and editorial assistance by Bonnie S. Egan
Printing by createspace.com

No work is ever created or completed in a vacuum. Our families have been patient when we went into our cocoons to write, and encouraging when we showed them the results. Time after time, edit after edit, when the words began to swim in front of our eyes, Charles' Tammy and Christopher's Vicky kept on encouraging us, knowing how much we cared about this project. Both of these wonderful women were and are great champions for us, and we love you.

We also are not ashamed to say that we love our clients—albeit in a different way. Thank you each and every precious one of you for entrusting us with your dreams, as we endeavor to make them come true, month after month and year after year.

To our colleagues, a deep and profound thank you and big virtual hug for dedicating your careers to providing quality financial advice. That kind of backup to the advice and counsel we provide is literally priceless. Please know that your support is deeply appreciated, on a daily basis.

Table of Contents

"*Power is the faculty or capacity to act, the strength and potency to accomplish something. It is the vital energy to make choices and decisions. It also includes the capacity to overcome deeply embedded habits and to cultivate higher, more effective ones.*"

STEPHEN R. COVEY, author (1932–2012)

"*We all woke up this morning and we had with it the amazing return of our conscious mind. We recovered minds with a complete sense of self and a complete sense of our own existence — yet we hardly ever pause to consider this wonder.*"

ANTONIO DAMASIO, neuroscientist (1944–)

Brain Science Illuminates How We Can Make Better Financial Decisions

HARVARD NEUROSCIENTIST SRINI PILLAY, M.D.

Y OUR BRAIN IS your central processing unit; it makes decisions for you. What decisions your brain makes is largely due to what you put into it. If you feed your brain nonsense, it will produce nonsensical advice. If, on the other hand, you feed it wisely and with care, it will produce beautiful and productive thoughts. That is why *Financially Secure Forever* is such an important book. On the one hand, it is a book about preserving and growing assets. In this day and age, that is certainly important. But as you read the book you will see that it is truly about you—and the things you might never have known about yourself in relationship to money.

Insecurity breeds uncertainty. Recent research shows that when we are in a state of uncertainty, we are more likely to think, like Henny Penny and her friend Chicken Little, that the sky is falling down. The reason uncertainty makes us anticipate a looming catastrophe is that it turns on the brain's two innate detectors: the "conflict detector" and the "gut-feeling detector," and turns them on far too high to give us an accurate reading. When your gut feelings become unduly negative, you get a stop signal even when, objectively, there is no reason to stop. With this chaotic start, messages become distorted. Your brain has gone into a state of excessive vigilance and will "jam on the brakes." When this happens often, it can create an uncertain life.

If this were just another fictitious Henny Penny drama that ends when you close the book on the children's fable, it would be less of a problem. However, uncertainty is contagious; it literally spreads. Apart from making us pessimistic on a personal level, our brains also spread this pessimism through a mechanism known as "mirror neurons." This is a system of connected brain cells that are strung together to mirror other people's emotions. Your neighbor's uncertainty can become your uncertainty in milliseconds without your being consciously aware that it is happening. The resulting fear can also continue to grow within you, below your conscious awareness.

So if you are not aware of it, why does it matter?

Fear, ambiguity and insecurity all activate yet another detector: the brain's fear detector, known as the amygdala. This critical brain region provides emotional input whenever we make decisions. Even when our fears or insecurity is subconscious, it can still activate the amygdala. In terms of how you make financial decisions, the problem is that the amygdala, your little but powerful fear center, is connected to the left hemisphere or thinking brain—that part of your brain where you would be making your financial decisions. If the fear center is overactive, it sends warning signals to the thinking brain that can eventually become extremely disruptive.

Let's say you have a medium-risk investment. If your brain is in insecure mode, this may appear to you as a high-risk investment. You may have stood to make a lot of money by taking an appropriate risk with this opportunity, based on your actual circumstances. However, your insecure brain may lead you to make the wrong decision. This is just one of the distortions that can and do happen in our brains when we feel insecure. In order to break the cycle of financial insecurity, it behooves us to understand this process, since, as in all things, knowledge is power and awareness can override instinct.

At first glance, the idea of thinking "seasonally" may seem unrelated to this body chemistry discussion. But when you really think about it, it makes good sense. For one, our thinking is influenced largely by our moods, and for many people moods vary by the season. It is no secret that the seasons themselves—cold or warm; raining, snowing or sunny—have a definite and genuine biological and psychological impact on our moods and therefore on our decision making. But that is not where the seasonal relevance ends.

Winter is the start of a new year, a renewal, the perfect time to conjure up ideal scenarios and adjust your investment profiles to help insure that your most important goals and dreams come true. The onset of Spring may have you restlessly trying to change your entire investment portfolio, more out of what the authors call "greed not need." This then is the perfect time to take a close look at your asset allocation to decide whether that balance still serves you, based on the goals and milestones you previously set in your Goal Tracking session.

Estate planning perfectly coincides with Summer, when we are usually in a more relaxed mode, perhaps spending more time with our families. And Fall is perfect for year-end tax planning.

Thinking about addressing your finances by season allows for a natural organization—a prompt that gets us into the mode to act. These are just some of the practical insights that you will be able to read about in *Financially Secure Forever*.

Most people agree that feeling insecure financially can be devastating. Most people know that planning and saving are optimal. Most people would say accumulating money for the future is a very good thing. This being the case, why then do most people not do this in ways that will best serve them? Is it laziness or a willful ignorance as in, "I'll deal with all this some other time?"

The answer is complex. When we need to change our habits—in this case, to start ourselves on a more proactive financial course—our brains are fine *thinking* about this. When we actually start to act, though, the brain goes into a state of what we call "cognitive dissonance"—that's psychological jargon for "brain chaos." Our brains love familiarity and habit, even when these habits are not good for us. There is very little the adult brain resists more than real change. People often change only when they are on the brink of disaster, and by that time it's usually too late. Before that, the brain is content to rearrange the deck chairs on the Titanic of your life, rather than urging you to jump overboard and in the process save yourself. In a sense, paradoxically, that is what *Financially Secure Forever* is telling us. It's telling us that we need not accept our current financial lives—that we can take charge. And it's telling us that we can do this in the context of each season, using this as a way to start and then maintain our best financial present and future.

What I'm saying is that it's hard to make real changes alone, and that when you utilize the Seasons of Advice process described in this book, your ability to change your financial future becomes infinitely easier.

What else, you may ask, is so special about Seasons? When you have a context that is constant and reliable, making a plan becomes much easier. We know from brain science that context is one of the most important factors to position the brain for starting new (and better) habits. Not having a context is also one of the most important reasons most of us never truly change. Conversely, when we anchor our actions to something that repeats itself over and over again, we give ourselves the gift of being able to rewire our brains with much more ease. It's like going on one of those airport "People Mover" conveyors that allow you to move forward with little or no effort. It's much easier to be on a conveyor belt moving safely forward than to try to find your way to safety completely on your own steam. The steps outlined in the book will take you all the way to safety with clarity and minimal effort because they have been so well thought out.

No plan, no gain, and maximum pain

The brain is wired for short-term reward and to discount the future. In fact, the brain's default mode is to feel rewarded by short-term benefits. It essentially has a hard time letting go of short-sighted changes that make us feel better. When we plan for long-term success, the brain starts to detour. How often have you decided, "Okay, this is it; I am going to take charge of my life"? And you have—except that a few months down the line you find yourself right back where you started. This brain phenomenon can create a "habit hell" because of the way brain cells work. Habit creates a chain of brain cells that fire together, automatically, in your habitual pattern. The key to getting your brain to change is to start a new habit by repeating the behavior consistently, especially at first. That this is possible is very good news and the basis for my conviction that this book could change your life.

Good news about change

The adult brain is capable of change. We call this neuroplasticity—the capacity of the brain to make changes to itself until it finds its way to where it wants to wind up. The trick here is that "where you want to go" has to be constantly outlined in your brain. Unless you have a constant reminder of a new habit, the brain will not keep your intention "online" and change itself willingly.

Just in case you're thinking at this point that perhaps you picked up the wrong book, this book is not about brain science. However, the advice it offers correlates with brain science quite remarkably. If you have an old bad habit, why not exchange it for a new good habit? There's not a more valuable natural system to anchor your good new habit to than the reliable year-round seasons described in the following chapters!

This is also a timely book on a global level. Never has the world been in such a contagious state of economic doom and gloom and out of control debt accumulation. I believe it's high time for us to stop this endless cycle and take charge of our financial lives. It's time to realize that if we do not, nothing is going to magically happen to help us grow or even retain our current assets. Most fortunes in the world have been built rather than inherited. Those who build them spend more time attending to what they can do rather than what they can't.

On your own, you probably can't do much about the global financial crisis. And on your own, you probably also can't do much about your own crisis. That is precisely why books like this are written. *Financially Secure Forever* was written by people who have come to understand what you most need to know in order to achieve permanent financial security. They know that a little smart guidance from experienced and caring professionals can make the difference that allows you and your family to meet your dreams and goals. Helping you do that is their passion and *their* goal.

After reading this book thoroughly you will have put your brain in exactly the right place at the right time. By the time your brain absorbs the knowledge, strategies and inspiration in these pages, you will be far better equipped to eliminate old ways of thinking and achieve the lasting financial security and success you want and, having worked hard for your money, also so richly deserve.

Good luck and happy reading!
Srini Pillay

Srini Pillay, M.D. is a humanist, an author and a pioneer in the field of neurocoaching—taking brain science out of the theoretical realm into the hands of business people.

ACKNOWLEDGEMENTS

This book had a "family" of important contributors, several of whom went beyond expectations by most generously sharing the story of their experiences with Seasons of Advice. Others in our professional family are people we work with daily and are the backbone of our consulting business, making it so much easier for us to do our jobs. In both those regards we specifically want to thank Edmond, Patty, Doug, Tom, Chuck, Sureita, Michael, Danny, Cornelia, Garry, Merle and Stan for their contribution to this book.

Our heartfelt thanks also goes to Ameriprise Financial Services for their commitment to excellence and steadfast commitment to supporting our clients. Bravo!

Finally to Judy Katz, our editor at Katz Creative Inc. Without her help in creating a logical flow, and her editing skills, this book would simply not have happened. Kudos to you, Judy, for helping us take this project over the finish line!

Financially Secure Forever

"It's good to have money and the things that money can buy, but it's good, too, to check up once in a while and make sure that you haven't lost the things that money can't buy."

GEORGE H. LORIMER, editor (1868–1937)

"It is not the strongest of the species that survive, nor the most intelligent, but the one most responsive to change."

CHARLES DARWIN, naturalist and author (1809–1882)

"No sensible decision can be made any longer without taking into account not only the world as it is, but the world as it will be."

ISAAC ASIMOV, scientist and writer (1920–1992)

Chapter 1

In a Rapidly Changing World, A New Financial Approach Takes Root

THE PURPOSE OF this book—the reason we wrote it—is to teach people how to think, or perhaps more accurately *rethink* the financial decisions they've made. At the same time, we wanted to share practical, useful rules, examples, and an actual *process*, for making better financial decisions. Together, the authors bring over 40 years of practical experience working with thousands of successful people and we have both had our share of industry awards and recognition. We have found that the best way to achieve your financial success forever is to have a process in place that systematically and proactively addresses relevant issues, has a clear focus and can be effectively coordinated with your other professionals.

To gain the insight, comfort and sense of financial security you need to produce the results you want, read this book with an open mind. We are proud of how effective the Seasons of Advice process has become over the past decade, putting thousands of people on the right financial track. From the enthusiastic feedback these "Seasoners" have provided, we are convinced this system can and will become a new standard in the industry. This is why, in addition to empowering you to put this system into play, we are equally intent on teaching other certified financial advisors how to bring this approach to the clients who trust them with their hard-earned assets and who deserve to be meticulously cared for—not once in a while, not hit or miss, but truly year-round.

As far as we know, Seasons of Advice® is the first financial management practice model developed for the public based on the relatively new disciplined study of neuroeconomics.

Unfortunately, in our experience a great many of the way financial decisions people make are disempowering. We can tell you, shocking as it may seem, that many people are so caught up in their day-to-day routines, and/or in the sheer "game" of accumulating capital, that they tend to focus almost solely on the numbers—how much comes in, how much goes out and how much they have in total. In the process, they seldom think carefully and accurately about how they will use their money and what they will really need it for in their near or even far-off future.

Understandably, we want our money to be there for us, help us do what we want, have what we want, go where we want, give what we want to others and, throughout the days, weeks, months and years of our lives, be able to always feel secure about all of it. Sadly, though, that is not always the way it works out.

Our intention is to give you a better understanding of key financial realities concerning your accumulated assets, your income and your future prospects for retaining and growing your assets. Regardless of whether your wealth comes from earnings, savings, inheritance or all of the above, we can say that if people understood these keys, far fewer men and women would lie awake at night worrying about whether or not their portfolios will keep pace with their goals and dreams.

This book is not a definitive behavioral textbook. We'll leave that to Dr. Pillay and others, but we will share our observations of what we have seen in terms of how people make the financial decisions they do. Good financial advisors try to learn what causes their clients to make their money-related decisions, or perhaps said differently, why clients react the way they do to the recommendations that are made.

Financial insecurity is a phenomenon that affects people across the board, and we can assure you that the affluent are not in any way exempt. Many comfortable or even wealthy individuals—yes, even some multimillionaires—privately admit to having at one time or another envisioned themselves as indigent. If you have this persistent sense of dread to any degree, you are certainly not alone.

As unlikely as this scenario may seem to be for those with significant assets, several large surveys have shown that the fear of running out of money is even greater than the fear of death! Given today's global socioeconomic uncertainties, this is less surprising than it has been in many years, perhaps decades. In truth, such fears have always festered in our collective subconscious, but in this time of volatile markets, it is logical to see why people feel deeply concerned. Very little, though, is widely reported about behaviors that would best help you personally to weather these storms.

A New Age of Super-Connectedness

Obviously, our world is significantly different than the world in which our grandparents grew up. We now have more people on the planet, all hyper-connected, whether they choose to be or not, with 24/7 news (most of it bad) from all corners of the earth. In the previous order of things, individuals, groups, countries, cultures and subcultures were in far less contact with one another, and therefore less able to influence each another. The world today, however, is a blended pot of interaction and reaction; everything connected with everything else in terms of trends, markets, currency, events, information, entertainment and cultures. All flow and mix like a strange new ecosystem.

To not only survive but actively thrive financially in such times, we must accept that the most important things in life simply cannot be predicted soon enough to be acted upon.

With this in mind, we need to intelligently develop processes that will help us make the right decisions at the right times. And we must do it in such a way that aims not to hoard money and assets but rather to invigorate them, to be able to decide what really matters to us, and to always be in a flexible position to respond to new investment and other financial opportunities quickly, creatively and effectively.

Overcoming a "Depression Mentality"

One thing we have often observed is that many people are subconsciously living their parents' way of dealing with finances. Their parents and/or grandparents lived through The Great Depression. This traumatic experience often informed their financial attitudes and fears, their standard of living, how they choose investments, their risk tolerance, how much money they choose to put away, and other aspects of their lives relating to money—which is actually all-encompassing.

This inherited, learned mindset is completely understandable; however, it needs to be excised. And it can be. With a few simple changes in the right seasons of response, anyone burdened with this limiting mindset can overcome it in order to create a prosperous, responsive yet stable financial future for one's self and loved ones. This is despite the undeniable reality of waking up many days (and hopefully fewer nights) to what may often seem a most difficult and unstable world.

CEO/CFO of You, Inc.

By the time you finish this book, you will have the information you need to be able to follow the Seasons of Advice® approach and become the Chief Executive Officer and Chief Financial Officer of You, Inc. The Seasons of Advice process will provide you with the background and tools to make the right decisions about insurance, taxes, estate planning, investments, etc. We are also giving you the opportunity to fully understand your personal decision-making process.

To that end, it is empowering to recognize when you are most rational in making any financial decision, and specifically whether that decision is based on your best interests or on less wise motivations. These insights can help you make better decisions for you and your loved ones and likewise help you set yourself up with the right structure and the right advisors for your financial well-being now and down the road. Overall, this new kind of financial planning can help provide better stability in the complex and shifting world we all live in today.

Not surprisingly, many people have trouble finding cohesive planning and advice. This is partially due to the fact that financial planning is actually a very young industry. Personal financial modeling was not well developed before the arrival and wide usage of desktop personal computers in the early 90's. Before that technology came about, the wealthy classes had a private family officer (PFO)—often a trusted family attorney or CPA who took care of everything, working with a host of other professionals. The family with assets of twenty five million to one hundred million dollars or more had nothing to worry about as long as this faithful retainer was loyal and honest.

Obviously, this is not a model for the majority of us today who aren't in these financial brackets. The good news is that the Seasons of Advice® process brings the benefits of a private family office service (a kind of "PFO Light") to more people, i.e. the "mass affluent" or high net worth individuals. These are generally people who are successful but not rich, with investable assets in the range of five hundred thousand to five million dollars.

Seasons of Advice creates cohesiveness

The emerging affluent, people with the kinds of assets mentioned above, are generally savvy people who may already work with various financial professionals. At the same time, these professionals may often be unaware of major blind spots in your overall financial planning that may leave you vulnerable. The beauty of the Seasons of Advice approach is that it also can systematically engage those professionals so you can enjoy the benefits of a more collaborative process.

For example, it is unrealistic to expect your attorney or your broker to proactively call you to find out if there are changes in your life that can affect your financial planning. It's simply not what these professionals do. Accountants are another example—they rarely call you mid-year to evaluate your tax situation. It's generally not what they do for most of us. Your insurance agent rarely calls you unless there is more insurance to sell. Your broker usually only calls when he has stock to sell you. The Seasons approach is holistic and delivers a proactive, systematic, relevant and coordinated approach to use, whether you are implementing the system on your own (with the help of this book) or with an experienced and knowledgeable advisor.

You know your accountant wants to do a great job for you, but if you don't reach out and tell her what life changes you have gone through since your last contact, how can she help you? Similarly, while your lawyer wants to keep your documents up to date and secure, he can only take action once he has the current picture. It is important for you to keep these individuals, your financial advisory team, apprised of changing events, such as a new job, a new grandchild, a change in marital status, health issues, etc.

Instead of thinking negatively about these professionals and what they do not do for you, the idea is to help them to more fully (holistically) understand your situation and your wishes. In this way, they will be far better able to help you accomplish your objectives—those that are truly in your best interests for both the present and future.

Following the Seasons of Advice strategies, you will address and examine the various components of your financial life.

This will allow you to better understand your risk tolerance and also what you really want your money to do for you. You will learn how to treat your advisors as if they were trusted colleagues.

Of course, we are each unique, but there are also common paths the human mind goes down, ways in which we think, feel and behave that fit into predictable patterns. These patterns can tell us a lot about particular individuals and how they make decisions about money: how they earn it, spend it, save it and share it. Understanding certain common patterns of thought and behavior, especially when it comes to deeply ingrained attitudes toward money and our conscious or subconscious, is important. Once you know yourself better, you will be able to work this program more effectively and, at the same time, progressively increase your comfort zone over time. One of the purposes of this book is to help remove much of the angst of financial planning. As you begin to see your past, present and future in a new light, a workable, organic, decision-making model for you and your family will emerge.

Part of the process is also helping you understand the way the mind works. As Dr. Pillay described in his Foreword, and as we will further describe in detail later on, it can be extremely helpful for you to know the type of person you are when it comes to making financial decisions. To that end, we will describe the Social Styles® models, which we have received permission to use here. The purpose of offering you these distinctions is to hold up a mirror to help you see which category you fall into most closely, be it *Driver, Amiable, Expressive* or *Analytic.*

These prototypes go a long way toward explaining why it may be quite easy for you to make certain life decisions, monetary or non-monetary, while you find other decisions extremely difficult to make. Many times those tougher decisions are simply left unresolved. This is an avoidance strategy that, in the area of your finances (and in other areas of life as well) can work against your hopes and aspirations, and derail your dreams.

In the go-go years before the dot com crash, before the irrational socioeconomic "bubble" burst, the market was going great guns. At that time, for many people, greed ruled, and even 100% was not enough of a return. People were making a lot of decisions mostly based on greed. Many had one idea in mind: maximum profit, in other words, getting more back on their stocks or bonds or dividends or other investments than the next person.

In the course of planning your financial future these days, understanding the basis for your decisions allows you to make them consciously and set in motion a wiser plan than you might otherwise adopt. In so doing, you will move your life agenda forward and won't get caught short of achieving your potential. You'll find yourself better prepared for whatever life brings, or, perhaps more accurately, whatever life springs! In truth, the only constant in life is change, which life teaches us is in every arena.

So now let's continue our journey as we share our own experiences and observations. The examples we provide are based on real situations and are being shared with permission, although names and some identifying details have been changed to provide privacy. You will most likely find in our examples many similarities to your own stories, goals and questions. These stories may help you understand your financial past and current needs and, in so doing, help you build a solid bridge into a very different financial future.

Getting to Know Yourself and Your Relationship to Money

1. Are you ready, willing and able to plan for the future? You need to be out of credit card debt and have an adequate emergency fund or cash reserve

2. Think about where your opinions about money come from: Family, Friends, Co-workers, Television?

3. How well and how often do you coordinate with your professional advisors like your accountant, attorney, investment manager, insurance agent?

4. Does worrying about money affect your family relationships or job performance?

We intend to answer many of these questions throughout this book.

"*Only one thing has to change for us to know happiness in our lives: where we focus our attention.*"

GREG ANDERSON, wellness author (1964–)

"*One learns by doing a thing; for though you think you know it, you have no certainty until you try.*"

SOPHOCLES, Greek playwright (496–406 B.C.)

Chapter 2

Getting to the Core of How We Make Financial Decisions

MOST FINANCIAL DECISIONS are made from a subconscious reservoir. Therefore, what may seem logical and intelligent to one person often seems illogical to another. People have vastly differing behavioral patterns and relationships to money. This has a lot to do with how they were raised and also how they made their money.

For example, growing up, you might have had parents who lived simply, even below their means, and kept money tucked away. Or, in contrast, you may have been raised in a family where your parents spent liberally. Although you lived quite well, there was no long-term financial security—but perhaps you really were not consciously aware of that. When we grow up, we often spend the same way our parents did, or we may rebel and spend our money in exactly the reverse way.

It's also very common for people to compare themselves to their friends and neighbors, paying close attention to the landscaping, cars and such so-called measures of success that others accumulate. There is no doubt we can be very influenced by others when deciding about purchases we make. Later, when we discuss social styles, you will see that there is actually a name for those that need to have the biggest and newest thing in their driveways and for the neighbors to see.

To really become financially secure forever, you need to become comfortable with making the right decisions for the right reasons. This chapter will give you insights into patterns you may have developed that can limit your ability to achieve your goals.

As we've mentioned, you should not underestimate the impact that societal and family history have on financial behavior. It's not a matter of wrong or right, but we repeatedly see people gauge what they should do against what they have seen from their parents, grandparents, friends or colleagues. In general, it's good to have a responsible framework. At the same time, remember to challenge yourself to be aware of what has changed in the world at large since that standard was set.

There are added factors and influences. Probably the most impacting is the fact that people live longer now and the vast amount of money that will be spent in a lifetime, especially in retirement years, is unprecedented—so much so that an additional dimension of planning has to be carefully considered as well. In addition, financial information is traded faster than ever today, and investment options and choices have increased. Computer models have been developed to track and predict performance, but these models may not comfortably align with your inherited beliefs or with your personal situation. These are all aspects that require individual assessment and insight.

Brain Function

Let's begin with some understanding of how the brain works. The relatively new science of neuroeconomics is actually a combination of several of the brain study disciplines that attempt to explain how individuals make economic decisions and address risk. It is a science that concentrates on several of the related sciences including psychology, sociology and behavioral economics to determine factors that influence economic decisions. The Seasons of Advice process has been highly influenced by this work and attempts to apply some of the understanding of the brain's tendencies to help you to a more direct and conflict-free pathway to proper and necessary ongoing financial decisions.

Researchers have undertaken the challenge of trying to understand why some people are comfortable taking risks with their finances and others are not. In many cases, the causes are hard-wired into the physiology of the brain. In other cases, emotions and feelings are the predominant triggers. A disturbing finding was that, if not framed properly, the brain may treat investment decisions similarly to the way it treats addictions, such as gambling or drug addiction.

The various functions of the brain play many parts in arriving at a financial conclusion and course of action. Decisions, even those we call "spur-of-the-moment" or "snap decisions" are really complex reactions to thought processes that involve multiple segments of the brain. Most people are aware that the right hemisphere of the brain is considered to be the more creative while the left hemisphere is the logical, scientific side. The right is based on emotion and intuition. The left side is more disposed toward clinical information and seemingly logical conclusions.

In 1861, neurosurgeon Pierre Paul Brosca discovered that the left and right hemispheres of the brain have separate functions. "Right-sided" persons are said to be emotion-dominant and are represented as creative, impulsive and intuitive. "Left-sided" individuals are more scientific and logical. It is said we all naturally lean toward either "right brain" or "left brain" dominant thinking. Some of us are more creative while others are more logical and calculating. In actuality, both types are simply imbued with a slight preference to one mode or the other. The state of the brain is not a static phenomenon. However "our consciousness is constantly evolving," as psychologist and philosopher William James from the same era reminds us.

The stereotypical characterization is not intended to be strictly applied, but it is helpful when we look at the financial decisions you will need to confront. The Seasons of Advice process tries to align these decision elements more naturally to the way the brain works.

The brain is divided into three major sections (although there are many subparts): Upper—the cerebral cortex, Middle—the limbic system, and Lower—the basal ganglia. The upper brain is where we reason; the middle brain is where we react to emotional impulses; and the lower brain regulates the functions of the body. Each of our Seasons is designed to target a specific area of the brain exclusively, which should help you make better decisions and avoid conflicts.

The mind operates at four predominant Brainwave States or Frequencies. These different states are classified according to the speed of the predominant brainwave signals from one neurological point to another at any one point in time. Although the brain stores and processes countless memories of experiences, events and data, your decisions are processed and made in sequential milliseconds. This speed and frequency is measured in "hertz," and the figures are obtained using an Electroencephalography (EEG) machine. You may find a description of these levels helpful.

1. Beta: This is where our minds usually operate in daily life. In such a state we have full conscious awareness of and attention to everything around us. Beta is usually typified by brainwave cycles of 15 to 40 Hz (cycles per second). Higher cycles of beta frequency usually equate to stress, anxiety and "over thinking" as the conscious mind becomes misguided or reacts negatively to a given situation. High brainwave beta frequency also equates to hypertension, increased heart rate, increased blood flow, cortisone production and glucose consumption. Generally speaking, you do not

want to experience the high beta state too often if you are concerned about your health, and it is definitely not a great state to be in when making important decisions.

2. **Alpha:** A mild daydream or light relaxation state. You are operating in Alpha when you become captivated with a good book and lose track of what is happening around you. Meditation is usually aimed at achieving Alpha, and in that state the brain operates between 9 Hz and 14 Hz. Alpha is typified by partial conscious awareness and partial subconscious predominance at the same time. Information is more easily absorbed when in Alpha; it is considered highly desirable for more effective studying. In Alpha states, the left side of the brain is used more for processing. It may surprise you to know that Alpha is the most optimal state for making financial decisions. Many people go into an Alpha state in the shower and report garnering great ideas. Unfortunately, it is a difficult place to write things down.

3. **Theta:** Deep relaxation where the conscious mind is, for the most part, "switched off" and the subconscious mind is left to flourish. This is usually typified by sleep, dreaming and very deep relaxation—clearly not the best frame of mind for our purposes.

4. **Delta:** Extremely deep relaxation/sleep with complete subconscious operation. Delta is experienced in the deepest level of sleep. It has been shown that the physical body recuperates at a heightened rate in Delta sleep. You can be in waking Delta if you are in an advanced state of meditation. Delta is typified by slow brainwaves at 1 Hz – 4 Hz. It is interesting to note that a skilled practitioner can, in Delta states, achieve such phenomena as not requiring anesthesia during surgery. This has been documented on numerous occasions

medically and scientifically. If we are to think of Delta as helpful for our purposes, it would be its ability to restore the body from stress, thereby creating more balanced thought and decision-making processes.

The Seasons of Advice process helps you move between the creative and the reasoned approach, resulting in balanced decision making. The process offers a focused set of tasks, techniques and decisions. It is a framework for your brain to stay in a more focused state. Taken as a whole, you will be better able to digest the financial realities and critical decision points because of a more efficient alignment with how the brain works. Avoiding conflicts of thought will make you feel empowered and confident. Seasons is a process that will make you feel financially secure.

Finally, there is strong data that shows us that the subconscious mind also plays a major role in decision making. The subconscious is far stronger than the conscious mind but unfortunately the subconscious tends to be more gullible. Logic may indicate one direction but your subconscious may try to influence you in the opposite direction. Some say that is where instinct comes from. Allowing your subconscious to weigh in but not to make absolute decisions makes those decisions more likely to be correct; yet many people allow their instincts to take a back seat, opting to transfer full control to the broker or professional.

But beware, the subconscious may also be unduly influenced by marketing messages and fear. Developing and trusting our instincts can also be one of the ways we can help the conscious brain make the right decisions. Either way, we should all endeavor to use as much brain power as we can muster.

Risk versus reward – portfolio selection theory

In the 1950's, the Nobel prize-winning economist Harry Markowitz, who we will further reference in Chapter 5 on Asset

Allocation, theorized the interaction between hope for gain and a variance of *"risk influenced economic decision making"* creating a foundation for portfolio efficiency. He established that the brain is able to analyze the degree of uncertainty in a probability distribution. Markowitz looked at several risk-taking decisions simultaneously and narrowed down his analysis to take into account only two variables: risk and volatility, which are also referred to as hope and variance. This made the process of revision and adaptation to different scenarios relatively simple. This would be the process the brain actually uses in repetitive decision-making contexts, when, for example, deciding whether or not to buy or sell a share of stock. It is a learning process that allows the brain to become more adaptive over time.

Men versus Women

It would be fun and very tempting to do a deep dive on the neuroscience of male versus female brain physiology but, quite frankly, the ultimate answer after careful evaluation is that, for the purposes of this book, gender differences really do not matter that much.

You will likely get a popular counter argument from others who will focus on the absolute differences, which there are. There will also be people who focus on those who may not have yet achieved a certain level of financial success or maturity. To be sure, these differences, while fascinating, most likely do not account for more than 10-15% of the differences we see in how men and women react to financial decisions.

As practitioners, we have not had to make notable changes to the way we generally present data and ideas on a strategic level to either male or female clients. What we do see is that once the decision to become financially responsible is made, especially for those successful individuals we expect to be reading this book, men or women, the brain's process is basically the same.

That said, there are definite differences in how strongly men and women may value one of the Seasons over another. An emotion-based Season such as the one that focuses on family and security seems to affect women a bit more deeply. But again this depends less on gender and more on the individual, their unique family history and specific concerns.

Men and women do have differences that make the journey a bit different. Women will tend to be more careful, and there is, in fact, definitely a fascinating testosterone versus estrogen conversation to be had. It has been observed that women have a slightly thicker corpus callosum, the structure that links the hemispheres of the brain, and this may make it a little easier for women to coordinate between them. Men's brains tend to be slightly larger but not used as efficiently as women's brains.

The prefrontal cortex of the brain, which transverses both right and left hemispheres, is where we are told decision making takes place. While it may develop differently in men and women in the earlier stages of life, by the time you finish reading this book, you'll have more than adequate ability to make the right decisions so long as your process is correct and your data relevant.

Finally, there is strong evidence that when they work on this together, men and women seem to make better decisions.

We try to help you understand why you feel the way you do about decisions throughout this book; however, ultimately, you do have to make them and keep moving forward. The Seasons of Advice model is your pathway to accomplish this.

Armed with this information, how do we train our brains to send us wiser and more astute financial information? On your journey to financial security, you will find that there is help along the way…keep reading!

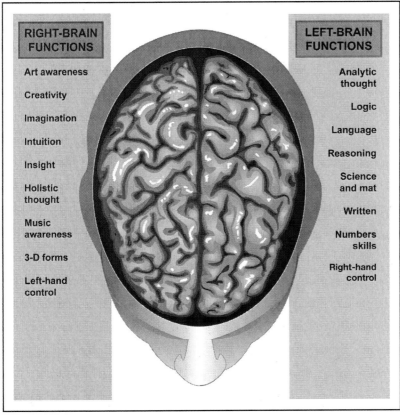

image © dreamstime.com

"*The cost of a thing is the amount of what I call life which is required to be exchanged for it, immediately or in the long run.*"

HENRY DAVID THOREAU,
naturalist and author (1817–1862)

"*He who hesitates is sometimes saved.*"

JAMES THURBER, cartoonist and author (1894–1961)

Chapter 3

Building a Secure Foundation

THE SOLID REASONS BEHIND THE SEASONS OF ADVICE APPROACH

BEFORE THE SEASONS of Advice process, most of the relatively sophisticated financial models the majority of financial professionals had to work with were somewhat geared toward the very wealthy. Unfortunately, it fit a narrow group of people—surely not the individuals we expect will find this book useful.

Successful individuals or families with investable assets between five hundred thousand to five million dollars, these core achievers, need a unique focus. They need models that can run financial details at their level, with a thorough yet time efficient process to proactively deal with the unique actions they must make to keep their family's finances and dreams on track.

People in this category must leverage their success without the benefit of the services of an expensive personal family financial officer. These "moderately wealthy" clients are typically well educated, well-read and able to understand a financial presentation and decipher a graph, chart or illustration. They can think on another level of complexity. It's what made them successful. They could be actively working or retired.

However, what they do need and may not have is an adequate financial decision model tailored to their requirements and a multidisciplinary *process* for proactively dealing with the need to make ongoing financial decisions, while clearly assessing their financial past and present and envisioning their future.

Making the right financial decisions that support critical life choices begins with a good foundation. Every day you make choices. To make the *right* choices, for the long run and not just for today, you need to first understand the emotions involved (as we discussed in Chapter Two) and then, in the right "Season," focus on the relevant proactive decisions assigned to that Season. It's like a really good chess player who constantly thinks several moves ahead.

Shortly we will review each season and the types of decisions to be focused on in each of those specific sessions. Also we'll discuss the prescribed order of these decisions, since they build upon each other as you move forward.

To effectively serve this group, we developed a formalized series of probing questions with decisions to be made on a regular basis that made sense for each family and met our high objective standards for sound financial planning. We designed this multidimensional process to accomplish our goals of excellent financial management and results while at the same time meeting the unique goals and needs of each client. As we refined our understanding and experience into a highly effective model, we achieved a system that not only takes into account how the brain works in the decision-making process but also provides a holistic platform for creativity and reason to work together collaboratively. This new process became known as the Seasons of Advice model or method.

The promise of the process, of course, is always the simple fact that it's all about having the money to do what you want when you want it and keeping it real—by which we mean balanced and realistic—with an acceptable probability of outcome.

Proactive, not reactive

The Seasons of Advice process, as it unfolds throughout the year, will not guarantee that your stocks will always keep growing or that your portfolio will never encounter losses. The severe market volatility over the last decade affected many people. While their portfolios fluctuated, this process kept them educated and engaged and ultimately kept them, and us, from making decisions based on knee-jerk reactions. Through the process they could stay proactive rather than making over-emotional decisions based on fear or short-sighted information. They could feel confident that they were still at the helm of their financial resources and not tossed about by the waves of change and sent drifting out to sea. This aspect of the Seasons of Advice process is always helpful in many ways, not least of which is calming nerves and assuaging concerns. Most important of all, staying proactive is the critical component in achieving financial security, both economically and emotionally.

An important thing to understand about the Seasonal process is that it is still a relatively new concept in the industry, even though it has now been in use for almost a decade. The reasoning behind the Seasonal model is simple: to promote financial understanding so otherwise successful people can feel confident that they have a process in place to manage, preserve and grow their assets. They learn that the process educates them and then supports them to do several important things: understand their own financial goals in a way they have not before, create a very real plan for meeting them, make timely, clear decisions and take wise actions that serve their dreams and goals. Over the years, as they move through the cycles again and again, they can adjust for the changes that life brings with new confidence about their long-term financial security.

The Seasons of Advice process brings one's entire financial picture together. It is a continuous proactive financial planning program that brings with it a deeper understanding that can help you make better, more relevant decisions. To be successful, financial decisions need to be made more quickly and more definitively than in the past. Since lack of time seems to be a common characteristic of most people, we needed a system that allowed for a laser focus on the right decisions at the right time.

It may be instructive to follow one couple we came to know as they were introduced to the Seasons of Advice program and began to see their financial lives and opportunities in a way they never could.

Marsha and Bill

When we first met with Marsha and Bill, it was Marsha who set up the appointment. "I feel concerned about our future, but confused about what actions to take," she admitted. "I'm not even completely sure what questions to ask. With all this 'noise' around us, we need to see the real picture and clearly understand the choices we need to make."

Marsha was an educated professional, an attorney who excelled at her profession and had achieved full partnership in her firm. Bill was a self-made success, the owner of a large manufacturing business. His business partner, Ray, had been with him for 20 years. "Ray joined me seven years in, just as we were starting to explode with success," Bill told us. "He's made all the difference. We're a great team and Ray's like family to us."

Bill had three children from his previous marriage, the youngest just starting her university studies. When they first came in, Bill and Marsha had other professionals who had supported them: a good CPA firm, an excellent bookkeeper, and a stockbroker. They'd planned, saved and invested reasonably well and, until recently, felt secure about their choices and actions. Now, however, it seemed their personal financial picture was growing shakier and more uncertain by the day. "We can't seem to see a clear strategy anymore."

"Our investments are really volatile," Bill said, "sometimes by as much as 30%." "It's a great concern," Marsha added. "We have a lot of questions about what to do about it, and we've had trouble getting clear advice." Specifically, they reported to have been given expert but conflicting advice from their broker and other professional advisors.

It was clear at the first meeting that Marsha and Bill, like many today, had begun to feel confused and a little paralyzed, fearing that this is "just the way things are," and that there is little they can do besides hope for the best. They felt the need to captain their ship carefully, but also felt they were somewhat adrift in uncharted waters. Should they stay the course or take risks, drop current investments and seek new? Was it time to conserve, change their lifestyle, retreat? Or should they perhaps sell off their other investments and put everything into real estate?

Many people today, whether male or female, married or single, self-employed or working for others, experience circumstances similar to that of Marsha and Bill. Similar feelings and questions come up as they watch what is happening in the markets and they become perplexed by the swirling changes and complexities of the world around them socioeconomically. They read and educate themselves, trying to act and react responsibly, but still don't feel they are seeing their way clearly.

First we asked Marsha and Bill some questions and listened carefully. In the process, we came to understand their financial lives, their hopes and dreams, as well as their frustrations and fears. We learned about their previous experiences, and we began to see what they were clear about and what they did not understand.

We asked Bill and Marsha to answer these questions: How much does it cost for you to live? How will that change in the future? What factors might cause that change? What might go wrong and how do you plan on preventing it? What investment options do you have? What is the tax effect of your income and expenses? What rate of return are you looking for and how much risk are you willing to take? There was a lot to absorb.

We explained that we had a process that standardizes the financial decisions that most successful people need to address on an ongoing basis and organized them into segments we called "Seasons." We also explained that each Season tries to align decisions based on a focused area of concentration in the brain—in other words, a neuroeconomic-based approach which could become a powerful tool to achieve financial security. It plays out like this:

1st **Season:** (Winter): Life goals setting and updates

2nd **Season:** (Spring): Investment strategies and asset management

3rd **Season:** (Summer): Family, security and intergenerational planning

4th **Season:** (Fall): Tax planning for today and tomorrow

We explained that the process, practiced in this order, eventually brings into focus almost every component of proper financial management, helping to do it in a relevant and meaningful way. As the normal flow of life occurs, financial decisions can now be comfortably introduced and re-introduced in a natural cycle. And, when unusual circumstances arise, such as a family crisis or career opportunity, there is always a current foundation upon which to rely to help make the right choices.

As it related to Bill and Marsha, it became clear to us that some of their goals were conflicting; some very real priorities had not been stated and others were as yet undiscovered. We could not recommend actions until they themselves became clearer about their dreams, goals and needs. As we explored and worked together, this began to change, and their picture started to get very specific.

Bill brought up his children: "It's great to really understand that my kids are already well taken care of; I think we're ahead of the game there. It's good to know that we can now actually focus on our own plans right away." Marsha chimed in that it was such a relief to her to know they could freely and with no guilt turn their attention to their own future and dreams. Realizing now that they did not want to manage or deal with properties beyond their own home, one investment property, and a family lakeside retreat in the mountains, they made some decisions about which properties to release in order to gain greater peace of mind and freedom from time constraints. "We originally thought we 'should' have investments in real estate and that we shouldn't sell now," Bill said. "We wanted to be smart about this. Instead, we are now able to understand what is really smart for us, for our goals, our picture." They both agreed they were not people who wanted lots of houses and properties. They were happy to let go of one of them.

Their real priorities, they said, were their careers. Each of them still had many goals for work—and for travel. "We love to work hard, and we balance that with great play too," Marsha told us. "Our travel with family and friends is one of our real priorities, but we haven't done it the last couple of years because we were worried about spending the money. We just weren't sure exactly how much we needed to economize so we stopped vacations altogether." In addition, they wanted to help certain family members who had health issues, and they wanted to make sure Bill's business partner and family were included in their thinking. They also hoped to establish a small family foundation to assist in providing certain assistance to people who were wheelchair confined.

Bill explained, "We both have family members who faced this decline as they aged. Because I work in manufacturing, I was able to engineer some innovations that made things easier for them. We'd like to offer this more broadly to others who face the same thing. It means development and manufacture in areas that aren't typically profitable, but it's something we feel committed to." Marsha agreed. "This really is a dream of ours."

As they worked through the Seasons, they came to realize the process must always begin with allowing yourself to truly dream, think clearly about your real happiness, allow yourself to break away from preconceived notions and develop new ones. When you are free from how you've been taught to be responsible about money or what your friends are doing or the world situation, you can begin dreaming your own dream. Then you learn how to align with who you are and what the life you truly want for yourself and your family is. Without freeing yourself up to visualize your real desires, you can make very poor decisions. This process expands your ability to realize your potential and gain more out of life.

Now let's go deeper and see how you can leverage the Season's of Advice® process and learn some new things that will help you make financial decisions in a more informed way.

Getting to Know Yourself Seasonally

1. Start making a list of the things you really want in your life today and in the long run for the **1st Season: (Winter):** Life goals setting and updates.

2. Think about what you need to learn and what questions you need to ask in order to make the best decisions for the **2nd Season: (Spring):** Investment strategies and asset management.

3. What would happen if there was a premature death or disability? Think about how well your family is prepared. Being prepared for contingencies is part of the **3rd Season: (Summer):** Family, security and intergenerational planning?

4. Evaluate your relationship with your tax preparer. Put a date on your calendar and start making a list of all the material you need for the **4th Season: (Fall):** Tax planning for today and tomorrow.

"Go confidently in the direction of your dreams! Live the life you've imagined."

HENRY DAVID THOREAU,
naturalist and author (1817–1862)

"Dreams pass into the reality of action. From the actions stems the dream again; and this interdependence produces the highest form of living."

ANAIS NIN, writer (1903–1977)

Chapter 4

Goal Tracking Season: Winter

TIME TO DESIGN THE LIFE
YOU *REALLY* WANT

S O, HOW *are* you doing? As we said from the onset, you are not alone if you are concerned about your money; it's something we humans all have in common, to varying degrees. To allay these fears, the Seasons of Advice process has been designed, and continues to evolve, in specific ways that have proven effective in helping others—and now you, the reader—to overcome the kind of money worries that can keep you awake at night. And, even more harmful, these fears can cause you to make some very bad decisions. Followed correctly, this system will put you (and your family) in a safer, more secure place with regard to your financial resources, emotionally as well as financially.

The Goal Tracking season sets a framework for the freedom to dream and keep on dreaming, like looking into a crystal ball and actually seeing into your future. You will envision what you want to see yourself doing, who you want to see yourself doing it with, where you want to be doing it, and how you can keep doing it for the rest of your life.

Personal enjoyment, enrichment and fulfillment leads the Seasons of Advice process. This would be aligned with right brain thinking. The right hemisphere of your brain is something you, as a unique individual, bring to this part of the process. It's hard for anyone else to creatively envision the future for you in the way you really want yours to be because it is so personal.

Let's take a look at the first of the four Seasons. The objectives of the Goal Tracking Season is to clarify all the assumptions you need to build a sound financial plan or revise your existing one. It is the guiding light of the Seasons of Advice process where you will develop the foundation for the other seasons.

Your annual Goal Tracking Season is a point in the early part of your year, every year, when you are asked to weigh your accomplishments, dream big, and evaluate your future challenges so you can envision and create the life you want. This may sound like an easy, fun activity; in practice, it is a real dilemma and emotional challenge for many people. By clarifying where you stand, you free yourself up to consider the following potentially life-changing decisions for you and your family.

- **Do you need to save more or can you save less?**
  What is the perfect amount to make it all work?

- **Do you need to change the timeframe for your goals?**
  Should you put off buying that bigger house or can you actually retire earlier than you think?

- **Can you add more goals to your financial life?**
  Better vacations, home renovations, etc.

- **How much do you actually have and where is it invested?**
  We find forgotten money all the time in old 401(k)s/ IRAs, bank accounts, stock certificates, life insurance policies.

- **What will your cash flow and expenses look like this year?**
  Can you make it on your net pay or do you rely on your bonus? When is saving easier? Monthly or annually?

- **Can you spend more money now instead of needing to save and still reach your goals?**
  Will it ruin everything if you buy that expensive pair of shoes?

- **Can you enhance your gifts to children, grandchildren or to charity?**
  Why wait until they are too old to use the money? And those grandkids were so cute today!

- **Are you taking too much or too little risk in your investments?**
  This is so important to know BEFORE the Asset Allocation Season.

- **Should you try to restructure your debt?**
  Are rates lower today? Would it make sense to borrow more or extend the mortgage? Perhaps pay off high loan rates instead of investing?

- **What is the proper amount to have as a reserve for emergencies?**
  Generally 3-6 months of your committed expenses.

- **What are the risks to your financial life?**
  Inflation. Rising interest rates. Stock market fluctuation. Business failures. Currency fluctuation and more.

So with all these things to think about, most people tend to miss the opportunities they very well can achieve. They don't know how far or how high to aim. They may not yet have the mechanics down to assess when they should start pushing, stop pushing, when to hold back or to go for it! Basically the whole intent of Goal Tracking is to *aspire to achieve and protect*.

You may need to learn a new way of thinking: thinking on multiple time planes (short-term, intermediate and long-term). The best solutions for short-term goals will usually be very different than the ones you would use for long-term ones. This can often derail plans for the future. Many times the numbers, the pure analytics, are too inhibiting. Dream and re-dream, because if you don't, things often stay the same or slowly erode.

In this season, stop obsessing about how well your stocks are doing and hold off stressing about taxes. Be optimistic and look at the glass half full. Let yourself focus on creatively envisioning your future. The ability to stop concentrating on the numbers and envisioning the future you want is easily the most critical part of living a successful life. Take your time and don't worry—our Seasons of Advice process will ultimately bring you through a natural process that will result in a realistic and actionable plan.

Financial calculators and assumptions

The scope of this book is not to teach you how to use financial planning software. If you do an Internet search, you can easily find an adequate quantity of tools you can learn to work with at reasonable prices. However, if you are not comfortable with all the components of a financial plan, do yourself a favor and consider using a professional to help guide you. In our opinion, you should only work with certified financial planners. There many advisors that claim proficiency in this area, but the CFP® certification or the CPA equivalent, the PFS, is suggested. And it's not only the financial analysis design where a professional edge will make a difference; acuity in implementing a plan is arguably a more important attribute. If you believe you have found the right people, trust them, but never authorize actions you do not understand. Finally, be clear on how they get paid. Later, in Chapter 11, we'll discuss more about working with a financial advisor if you so choose.

Remember that although it is emotionally driven, proper financial planning is ultimately a math exercise. Like every math problem, the key is to understand all the relevant assumptions, the variables and how they relate to one another. Clarifying your current thinking with regard to these assumptions and your most current choices is what you need to accomplish in the Goal Tracking Season.

These assumptions should include presumptions around inflation, tax rates, life span, future real estate buys and sells, changes in spending that will result from children leaving the roost, and rates of return presumed on your investments. You need to decide today which of your current assets are earmarked for which specific goals. What does the future hold for income, either from working, pensions, government programs, etc.? Of course, there's much more to consider.

It's surprising how many people really have no idea of the power of their finances. We know a woman in her late sixties who is an excellent, if extreme, example of this phenomenon. This woman is quite well off. When she came to us, she had more money than she could probably spend over her lifetime. She was on the boards of several charities and was a very giving and caring person, always thinking of others.

One day she came in to our meeting pretty upset, telling us how she had to take two buses to come to us and both were delayed. We told her next time she should consider taking a taxi which would be far more convenient and that she could certainly afford it. At first, she protested; with her frugal upbringing rooted in a depression era mentality, this was wasteful and, even perhaps, shameful.

The next time she came in she proudly told us, "You'll be happy to know that I took a cab here." She was happier and her long-term financial security was not compromised. This is similar to those who clip coupons and keep them in the glove compartment of their luxury sedan. If they want something and they can't find the coupons, they don't buy it. It's a great discipline and probably is part of the reason they are financially secure today, but eventually you need to reap the benefits of this lifetime of responsible behavior. The Goal Tracking Season is where you give yourself permission to do so.

Then there's just the opposite: unencumbered, red zone spending. Is this you or someone you know? Do not let credit card companies take advantage of you with sky high borrowing rates. If you can't pay for it in the current billing cycle, don't buy it! (Thank you, Suze Orman)

So, let's get going

So yes, start with your vision. Then it's time to tackle the rest of the assumptions. We chose winter for Goal Tracking because it is the time when the New Year presents itself, when we make our New Year's resolutions. With a fresh new year lying ahead, this is the most logical time for you to assess where you stand.

The first task in Goal Tracking Season is to establish your cash flow. First anticipate what is going to come in from your income and out from ongoing expenses and overhead, as well as projected outlays for major projects for the year, such as home improvements, travel, tuition, or any other big plans. Once your base is set, you can adjust for things that might change in the future. Remember, all investment and tax decisions you will make in future seasons will reference back to this information so it's important to get a good picture. Don't obsess about it though; you'll revisit this later in the year and make refinements, so its fine if it's close but not exact. And never refer to this as a *budget*. We hate that word because it implies that you should not deviate from your plans, which is the opposite of financially secure.

Can you live on your base income? It would be good if you can target any extra income or cash flow to savings. This would include bonus payments and company stock awards if you are working, as well as tax refunds. At the end of this chapter, we will give you a checklist you may find helpful to organize this information.

A word about Greed vs. Need

In the process of Goal Tracking you are going to have to begin to understand some of your core drivers or natural tendencies. In other words, what is your underlying agenda, your *real* motivation for what you want to do, to buy, to *be*? That is also where we define **greed** and **need** distinctions. You **need** anything that will result in your achieving your stated goals. That is what **need** is. For example, you have a goal and in order to afford to achieve it, you agree to a certain level of risk. If you get greedy and take more risk just for gain, and not to complement your goals, you'll more than likely repeatedly go off track. You have moved into **greed** territory. You are no longer in control. Your goals, which are born from your dreams, should create a kind of North Star for you to navigate by. **Greed**-driven decisions may take you off course more often than is healthy.

Keep in mind that pure **greed** is driven by adrenaline, competition etc., not the North Star of your goals. This deviation may work in the short run, but over time you will go off course if you are not true to your longer term goals.

The issue here is not whether **greed** is good or bad. From our standpoint **greed** is only bad if it puts your lifestyle and your future at risk if things don't work out. That is exactly why Goal Tracking is so critical to the process: it clearly identifies **need**, right from the outset. On the other hand, if a proper foundation for **need** has been established and confirmed through Goal Tracking, **greed** is certainly not a problem because it will not threaten your needs.

Daniel was 42 and had no patience for traditional investing. Interestingly, he worked as a parachute-jumper firefighter (they're called smokejumpers). He had a highly paid, high risk job, yet his stated goals and dreams were very simple: he wanted a modest, paid-for house in the suburbs with a pool and a yard to entertain his buddies. He wanted his two children, who lived with his ex-wife, to have good educations, and he wanted no debt and low overhead. Understandably, he also did not want to be a burden to anyone when he was old.

These were good goals for him. He made good money and could reach these through his income and savings alone but he liked to trade "penny stocks" hoping to make "big money." However, this plan did not work out for him. His financial risk-taking was probably more about his adrenaline-based work style. In his financial world, it translated into greed because it wasn't aligned with his goals, and he was taking on too much risk. It wasn't who he needed to be in his financial life. He later said that this was very illuminating for him and that it dramatically changed his outlook. Ultimately, he realized that his financial persona and his private persona needed to be different.

Choosing your personal path

Most financial planners come from an analytic background, so they speak analytically. They love their ratios, pie charts, graphs. Those are important but should be secondary to the power people have within themselves to shape their future. Goal Tracking starts with your dreams, the goals—the longed for *what, where, when* and *with whom*. When you can assess this, you will know whether or not you need to add to or modify your goals. It's an important and ongoing discipline.

Think of Christopher Columbus. He set out to reach a particular place. Where he ended up was not where he expected, but he did keep steering the ship. In the end, he and his crew wound up in a far better place. An alternate scenario, one that's all too common, is that when situations change, as they invariably do, you panic and try to fight the current, wasting valuable time and resources. What you really need to do is what Goal Tracking season requests you to do. You don't put it on autopilot. You keep steering your ship, even when you feel you are lost at sea. You will continue to make adjustments.

If you do this, the likelihood is that, like Columbus, you will reach someplace wonderful, even more exciting and fulfilling than the place you were originally headed for.

Maggie

Maggie is someone else we knew. She was very concerned about what would happen to her family if she got laid off. She was married, had just turned fifty, a very successful executive at a large company, and she was the primary breadwinner in the family. She was a higher-end middle manager, but given current conditions, she wanted help determining what the damage to her lifestyle would be if she got fired. We went with a worst case scenario. What we found out was that if she could stay in this job for another two years, she would then be crossing the line into financial independence. We looked at severance, insurance, savings, investments, inflation, taxes and the entire picture. We looked at everything with her clear goal to be solid if she lost her job.

Because she got a clear picture of how her income worked with everything else, her stress level receded. We were able to forecast that she would not have to change her lifestyle. What we saw was that in two years she would have the security she needed. Security was a huge priority, which is why she was so concerned about the possibility of losing her job.

As those two years passed, we adjusted our investment approach. Had she said she wanted to retire at sixty, ten years later, we would have created a different scenario. On the other hand, we increased her cash reserves and short-term bond positions significantly, in case she needed money sooner.

That was a while back and, unfortunately, she did get laid off when she was fifty-five. But by then she had worked for more than the two years needed, which put her ahead of her goal, so she was well prepared. We had continued to goal track all those years, watching the environments, the job markets, and encouraging her to dream up new goals.

Dreams don't have to be big dreams in order to be rewarding and provide peace of mind. Sometimes we ask, "If you won the lottery today, what would you do differently?" Surprisingly enough, the vast majority say they would not make many major changes, perhaps buy a bigger house, pay off debts, etc. but not really change their lives to a great extent. Of the others, the major changes people say they would make are related to helping their families or the needy.

This has happened many times in Goal Tracking meetings. We look at someone's goals, which might encompass going on an exotic vacation, and we see that they are ahead so we tell them, "Okay, you now have the opportunity to take that wildlife safari to Africa or that cruise around the world." Sometimes they take the trip, and sometimes they decide they now want to change their goals and instead build toward something else, for example, making down payments on homes for their children. It's nice to have a set time to evaluate these decisions.

To be able to plan and prioritize, you need to determine what's important to you. Only after playing creatively with your own ideas will you learn what excites you and why. This is a classic right brain activity. Start the year by considering all your choices, choosing clear priorities and goals and reevaluating your risk tolerances. Then you will be well prepared to move forward. Yes, numbers and data inform that process, but they are not the place to begin. This now brings us to the next of the Seasons of Advice—Asset Allocation. Turn the page, and let's head toward the Spring Season, where we take a look at your ideal mix of stocks, bonds, cash and collectibles.

Sample Expense Sheet

Feel free to download a copy with our compliments at our website:
www.Financially-Secure-Forever.com

Annual Expense Estimates	Amount	Frequency	Annual Amount
Housing			
Mortgage			
Real estate tax			
Association fees (townhome, condo)			
Rent			
Utilities (electric, gas, water, etc.)			
Internet / cable / satellite TV			
Home improvement			
Home maintenance / repairs			
Lawn or snow services			
Housekeeping			
Homeowners insurance premium			
Umbrella insurance premium			
Food			
Groceries			
Dining out			
Medical expenses			
Medical / dental / vision premium			
Medical expenses			
Prescriptions			
Alternative medical treatments (chiropractor, massage, etc.)			
Transportation			
Auto insurance premium			
Auto lease			
Fuel			

continued on next page

Annual Expense Estimates	Amount	Frequency	Annual Amount
Transportation (cont.)			
Auto maintenance (oil changes, repairs, etc.)			
Auto licensing (license plates, vehicle tax)			
Parking / tolls / bus / taxi			
Future/replacement vehicle (note: also specify the Start and End dates in the Frequency section)			
Entertainment			
Hobbies			
Children's activities			
Recreation			
Tickets (music, movies, events, etc.)			
Travel			
Other entertainment			
Personal			
Education costs (note: also specify the Start and End dates in the Frequency section)			
Dependent care / in-home care (note: also specify the Start and End dates in the Frequency section)			
Financial planning services			
Professional services (tax preparation, attorney fees, etc.)			
Clothing			
Phone(s)			
Home décor / furnishings			
Household supplies (Target, Costco, Wal-Mart, etc.)			
Personal care (hair care, spa, dry cleaning, etc.)			
Gifts charities			
Gifts to family and others			
Allowances			
Memberships and dues (e.g., gym, clubs, professional)			

Annual Expense Estimates	Amount	Frequency	Annual Amount
Personal (cont.)			
Subscriptions			
Unreimbursed employment expense			
Miscellaneous			
Other Expenses			
Alimony			
Child support			
Pet care (vet, grooming, pet food, etc.)			
Life insurance premium			
Disability insurance premium			
Long term care premium			
Other			
Grand Total			

"Clear thinking requires courage rather than intelligence."

THOMAS SZASZ, author, professor of psychiatry (b. 1920)

"To give away money is an easy matter and in any man's power. But to decide to whom to give it and how much and when, for what purpose and how, is neither in every man's power, nor an easy matter."

ARISTOTLE, Greek philosopher (384–322 B.C.)

Chapter 5

Asset Allocation Season: Spring

TIME TO MIX STOCKS, BONDS, CASH, COLLECTIBLES

AS EACH SEASON builds on the next, market conditions affect the value and composition of your portfolio, as do other factors that we will discuss later in this chapter. The overriding consideration for asset allocation should be based on the parameters and the assumptions you just set during the Goal Tracking season.

We are complex creatures, especially when it comes to money, a highly emotional issue. We have seen that money matters can have dramatically different meanings for different people, depending on their upbringing, aspirations and personal situations—all of which can also change with the ebbs and flows of each life. So the investment equation is not always as simple or straightforward as it could be.

Goal Tracking, the first Season of each year, becomes the foundation for what happens in your annual Asset Allocation exercise, as opposed to trying to time the market at various times throughout the year.

In the Goal Tracking Season, as we described in the previous chapter, you'll shun strategies about making as much money as possible and turn them toward specific *goals*. You have created these goals to be as specific as possible, including specific timeframes and benchmarks. Each person's needs and wants are individual, and the structure of investments, holdings and overall portfolio can take many forms, but there are basic fundamentals that define the propriety of most investment strategies. The most relevant of them is *time*. This is the critical determinant of asset allocation as far as we're concerned.

The next step is negotiating realistic expectations, in other words, reconciling a needed rate of return with a comfortable risk profile. It's not that easy. You may need to earn 7.8% on your holdings to achieve your retirement targets, but you're also having difficulty sleeping at night knowing your portfolio can fluctuate. It's almost impossible to have both. It's time to face up to the acid test. Can you compromise one for the other, return for risk, or better said, return for volatility? If you're the type to store big balances in a money market fund because you value safety above all, you may have a problem making the puzzle work. It's not necessarily a wrong decision but, of course, money markets often do not produce anything close to a 7.8% return, which means there is a disconnect here.

While the Goal Tracking process aligns with right brain functions—your dreams, goals, things like that—the second Season, Asset Allocation, the focus of this chapter, is more left-brain oriented, more tactical and practical.

Re-optimizing an unbalanced portfolio

When creating a portfolio, you should start with a core asset allocation model that is specifically earmarked for a specific goal, for instance, retirement or college education. Modern portfolio theory will have you use many different asset classes to try to balance the risk and reward. This is called diversification of asset classes and is a core principal.

Asset classes are general categories of investments like small company stocks, large company stocks, intermediate bonds, international bonds, cash, real estate, etc. In this Season your objective is to set the perfect mix for your portfolio. Then, on a recommended annual basis, you should rebalance the portfolio, which we also refer to as re-optimization.

In broad terms, asset classes would be equities, fixed income and cash equivalents. Equities are stocks, real estate ownership, cars and collectibles, such as jewelry or art—in other words, anything tangible in which you have ownership. In fixed income, you have bonds and other investments that pay good dividends or interest. From there it breaks down even further. For example, stocks can be broken down into foreign investments, US companies, large, mid and small, while fixed income bonds can be broken into corporate, government, international and tax exempts.

How do you know what class the asset is in? If you are just not sure what classification your asset is in, one easy way to find out is to simply go to a site such as Google® Finance and enter your ticker symbol. If the market capitalization is under $2 billion, it would be a small company (believe it or not). Between $2 and $10 billion would be mid-cap, and over $10 billion would be a large cap. If you are trying to classify a mutual fund, the same site will actually quote you the Morningstar® classification which is good enough. Diversifying among many companies in the same business or industry is not diversification because it doesn't cover enough different classes of assets.

In designing a portfolio, you need a mix of just about everything. This is called a diversified portfolio. The more bonds the more stable, the more equities or stocks, the more volatile. The former, the bonds, yield generally lower returns over the long run. The latter, equities, can yield better returns but get ready for the ride!

Depending on your need, more of your holdings might go into equities or more might go into fixed income or cash. There is no doubt equities are riskier. It's generally a set rule: the higher the ability to tolerate risk, the more money can go into equity investments. Lowering the risk means going more heavily into fixed income and cash. Once your perfect mix is created, you will rebalance the portfolios annually each time the Asset Allocation season rolls around.

The act of rebalancing investments is the action of bringing a portfolio that has deviated away from one's target *asset* allocation back into line. Underweighted securities can be purchased with newly saved money; alternatively, overweighted securities can be sold to purchase underweighted securities.

Let's say your plan for the previous year was to have 60% stocks, 30% bonds and 10% cash. Now we look at what happened throughout the year. Depending on the market, that 60% stock portion could have risen on its own to 70% because stocks may have performed exceptionally well, or it could have gone down. Each year you will make adjustments to get back into balance. Of course, all this also depends upon what is going on in your life as well as what's happening in the outside world.

Let's say your target rate of return was the 7.8% for the overall portfolio. What happens a year from now if those percentages were not met? The portfolio might have to be restructured to create a different type of return the next year. That will become necessary because the goal is, as we said, the North Star that guides us might—no, will definitely—require us to make adjustments as we go. This is what the Asset Allocation Season is all about. You may need to rebalance that portfolio to get back into alignment, take profits off the table if you are up and buy things at a discount if you're down.

The key is to do this at the same time every year. This is your Spring activity. Also, as a general rule, you should try to keep your assets flexible, possibly opting for investment structures that allow you to make changes at little or no cost.

Now let's revisit risk tolerance. For most people, this is a real wakeup call. If you need to earn 8% and an 8% portfolio means that you have to have 80% in stock and 20% in fixed income, you may have to live with a portfolio that could fluctuate significantly, perhaps as much as 20% in either direction. How do you feel about that? You could do well, but it would be very volatile.

Instead of trying to time the market, you need an objective process, a point in time to assess risk tolerance and to accurately determine whether or not one can accept the portfolio needed for your goals, notwithstanding the volatility. Someone might inherently be conservative in nature, or just the opposite. If you are conservative but you need to earn a higher rate of return, are you willing to live with the volatility? All investment scenarios must "pass the sleep test." This means, can you go to sleep at night without worrying about your portfolio?

We have included a risk assessment profile at the end of this chapter which can also be found online at our information site. This assessment poses such questions as these: "If your portfolio dropped more than 20% in a six-month period, how would you feel? How would you react? Would you sell everything?" Some people say "Yes, I would sell everything." Here's the thing: you should never be in that situation. If you are, it means that you were not correctly advised and your portfolio will not hold up. This is panic selling, and what it leads you to is counterintuitive—you will be selling low and most likely buying back in when prices are high. That is definitely not what you want to be doing. The Seasons of Advice approach is to set yourself up to prevent that as much as humanly possible by taking an objective time for rebalancing.

Timeframe is important

Of course, a question that often comes up is, "How long should I wait to sell if I've lost money already, and we don't know if the market will drop more at some future point?" Historically, over varying periods of time, markets do tend to come back, if not always as soon as necessary. That's the dilemma. That's why part of the portfolio structure we need to take into account is timeframe, and timeframe is based on your age and when you need a given amount of money for a given purpose. This, in turn, dictates how that portfolio should have been structured in the beginning.

Another question we are usually asked is: "How much cash should I have?" For argument's sake, let's say that as part of the planning process you want to make sure you are protected against short-term emergencies, like a job loss, major car repair, or perhaps an unexpected medical bill. You also want to have some money on hand for unusual opportunities. We think you'll want about six months' worth of committed expenses as a cash reserve. Bank deposits and shorter term government bonds would be good investment vehicles for the cash reserve.

One of the benefits of having different types of investments in your portfolio is that this makes it easier to not get emotional and make a fear-based "Just sell everything and get me out" decision. Now you have time. When things are happening in a dramatic fashion, it's often difficult to react rationally.

A big factor in the Asset Allocation Season is where you are in your life financially. Are you still working and, if so, is the money you are earning paying your overhead? Or did you already achieve retirement? If you are retired, part of what you need your portfolio to do is help recreate your paycheck.

Someone who is no longer earning but now requires income from their portfolio is in a different position than someone still earning and building income. If you are taking income, your focus is likely in areas that are creating dividends and interest; thus you would want a bigger portion of money in stable areas. This would mean you would not necessarily find yourself in a position where you had to sell your stock positions, which could be down at the time, to cover your cash needs. In that scenario, your asset allocation structure would be very different from that of someone whose income is still growing and savings are still accumulating. In the volatile markets, you generally should not sell, but rather try to hold on.

We know a couple who are in a really good place because they have more money than they really need. As markets performed well, they continually lowered the overall risk in their portfolio by reducing equity positions, using more fixed income, more hedging and other alternative strategies. When the market did adjust downward, they didn't have as much in equities (stocks) because they were taking profits off the table as they could.

While there is no perfect portfolio—no *one size fits all* that you can just adopt as your own—there are specific types of portfolios that fit similar circumstances. But be aware that once you set your model it usually drifts and will eventually be out of balance again to some extent. That's one of the reasons a proactive process like the Seasons of Advice model is needed.

So set your Asset Allocation in the spring and then let it alone. Try not to tinker with it too much, leaving most adjustments to simple asset class substitutions, such as replacing one small cap fund for another throughout the year, if you feel it necessary. Try not to change your diversification until the next Asset Allocation Season in the following spring. In the long run, you should be better off.

Customized asset allocation is best, but here are some very general examples

If you're in your 30's, we will expect to see about 80% stock, 20% fixed income. If you are in your 50's, it's more like 60% stock, 40% fixed income. And, if you are in your 70's or older, you might find it closer to 20% stocks, 80% fixed income. These are examples of "model portfolios" which most investment houses have to offer. They are not as sophisticated as the customized portfolio design a professional can do for you but will keep you in the general area of correct choices. You can request an appropriate model portfolio for each of your goals from your investment custodian.

However, this does not work for everyone. There are people in their 70's for whom these percentages, 20% equities, 80%

bonds would not give them enough income to maintain their lifestyle. Unless you have many more assets than you would ever need, most people do require a slightly more aggressive portfolio to take care of themselves and their loved ones for their entire lifetime than they would normally have in a model portfolio. Remember, it's always about choices.

A successful business owner we know has an excellent net worth. He is comfortable and does not need to take unnecessary risks. He is still actively working and making a lot of money, and, for the most part, his portfolio is conservative. He has put most of his money into real estate and tax exempt bonds. He bought a premium apartment in the city and has a luxurious home in the country, both of which are a part of his net worth. He does not have a need for a significant position in stocks so he chooses not to allocate a large percentage to equities. He retains his wealth by staying aligned to his goals, not by playing the many ups and downs. He has chosen to align his portfolio with a risk level aligned to his goals and current financial well-being. This is a good example of aligning his asset allocation to his Goal Tracking season.

Once you create a core portfolio, you may be tempted to add certain alternative investment vehicles, such as hedge funds, commodities, structured products, currencies and others, but these are the things that require the utmost education. Tread carefully. As we've mentioned *greed* is too powerful. You can see it in play when people go from "I don't want to lose any money" to "Why aren't we making more money?" almost overnight! We have often seen people reverse the pendulum from seeking more conservative investments after markets go down (when it's too late) and agreeing to more risk after the markets have risen (when it's too late).

Things move too fast and instincts cannot be solely relied upon. That is why an objective time of year for rebalancing is your job in Asset Allocation. When your Goal Tracking Season has determined you have more money than you need, you can be more conservative and you don't have to design your allocation to get higher rates of return—which, of course, will have more risk.

As you complete your annual Asset Allocation Season you will have created and refreshed the perfect portfolio to support your goals while staying within your risk tolerances. You will have set your performance expectations and rebalanced your portfolio to a proper diversification. Of course, nothing happens in a vacuum and our ever-changing world will always bring new considerations as you make your investment decisions, but try to not overthink your options. Following the prescribed asset allocation models should work out well for you if you match the timeframe and risk appropriately, and you surely can.

It's time now to move on to the next season, a different experience once again that can be somewhat emotional and introspective, and that's a good thing.

Risk Tolerance Questionnaire

1. Do you agree that in order to get a high return on a long term investment you must be ready to accept an annual return that varies greatly?

   a) Strongly agree

   b) Agree

   c) Somewhat agree

   d) Disagree

2. What are the goals for your investments?

   a) To grow aggressively

   b) To grow significantly

   c) To grow moderately

   d) To grow with caution

   e) To avoid losing money

3. Would you sell off your investments if you face a loss of twenty-five percent in your investments within one year?

a) Yes

b) Maybe

c) No

4. Do you use the interest and gains from your investments to pay your bills?

a) Always

b) Often

c) Sometimes

d) Rarely

e) Never

6. How concerned are you about losing money from your investments?

a) Extremely concerned

b) Very concerned

c) Concerned

d) Slightly concerned

e) Not concerned at all

8. How much interest would you have in taking risks to get higher returns on investments?

a) Very interested

b) Interested

c) Not interested at all

Use the previous answers to help you determine the appropriate risk level for you as defined below:

Conservative: I am only willing to accept the lowest fluctuation in account value in exchange for a relatively low risk/return potential. I understand this portfolio could still experience a decline in value of 5% or greater in any one year. This would mean very little or no equities in the portfolio.

Moderately conservative: I am willing to accept a relatively low fluctuation in account value in exchange for a below-average return potential. I understand this portfolio could still experience a decline in value of 7–10% or greater in any one year. This could mean as much as 25% equities in the portfolio.

Moderate: I am willing to accept an average fluctuation in account value in exchange for an average return potential. For example: I am comfortable with an exposure of up to 50% in equities and understand this portfolio could experience a decline in value of 20% or greater in any one year.

Moderately aggressive: I am willing to accept a relatively high fluctuation in account value in exchange for a relatively high return potential. For example: I am comfortable with an exposure of up to 75% in equities and understand this portfolio could experience a decline in value of 30% or greater in any one year.

Aggressive: I am willing to accept the highest fluctuation in account value in exchange for the highest return potential. For example: I am comfortable with an exposure of up to 100% in equities and understand this portfolio could experience a decline in value of 40% or greater in any one year.

"A big part of financial freedom is having your heart and mind free from worry about the what-ifs of life."

SUZE ORMAN, financial media professional (1951–)

"The future belongs to those who believe in the beauty of their dreams."

ELEANOR ROOSEVELT, stateswoman (1884–1962)

"Whoever wants to reach a distant goal must take small steps."

SAUL BELLOW, Nobel Prize-winning novelist (1915–2005)

Chapter 6

Family, Security and Intergenerational Planning: Summer

TIME FOR FAMILY DECISIONS

S O FAR WE'VE explored the core foundational elements in building your financial plan. By taking an approach based on neuroeconomics, we were able to correlate the concentrated mapping of financial planning tasks with the way the brain works. We have explored dreams and goals and designed a framework to implement investment strategies in a sound and relatively secure way—the former focusing on the creative thinking part of the brain that is mainly featured in the right hemisphere. We then turned to the left analytic hemisphere and dedicated the second season to asset allocation. Once again, let us remind you that the order in which you take on each season is critical. Let's now focus on protecting yourself and your family against challenges that go beyond investment risk and inflation.

Unfortunately, there will always be death, disability and potential long-term incapacity that can not only derail your financial security but could also put your entire family at risk for generations to come. How you feel about protecting your family, and the gratification you get to know that you have done the right thing to safeguard them, is what this next season is all about.

We also suggest that you use the summer months to check in on your cash flow. Hopefully, it's going the way you expected.

You'll need to be clear on your family's spending patterns before the next Goal Tracking Season rolls around. You don't want to get halfway through the year and find yourself in trouble because you haven't been following your own plan, or that you have been derailed by unexpected expenses. Part of this preparedness is to always have a cash reserve for emergencies or opportunities. That brings us to an important discussion on other risks.

All too often, financial plans stop at investment strategies. But consider how a premature death or suddenly losing your ability to do your job or run your business would, in almost all circumstances, endanger any financial security you may have. To effectively deal with these concerns and the choices you need to make, we have dedicated the third season of your financial year to Family Security, or what is sometimes referred to as Intergenerational Planning. This is where you will focus on the sometimes complex "protection" issues and the emotions that are always present when dealing with family. We will explore the basic financial documents you will need to have like Wills, Power of Attorney, Health Care Proxies and more.

The objective of the summer planning season is to make you feel secure so that you have the clarity to think and re-think how such things as insurance and estate planning decisions will impact the whole family, should one of these life events come to pass. Hopefully, you will never have to deal with these issues, but unfortunately many do. Before you go out and buy insurance policies, we believe there are some basics you need to think through.

Preserving your lifestyle with Life Insurance

The focus of the conversation about life insurance is really about maintaining a certain lifestyle, should someone prematurely pass away. It also means that the family would still be able to accomplish such major life goals as college tuition for a family member and even retirement for the surviving spouse.

That is not to say there aren't other very appropriate reasons to have life insurance. We will explore the investment and tax benefits later in this chapter, but from a need-based standpoint, your priority should be to get the right amount of coverage to preserve your current lifestyle, plus enough for other major expenses. We'd also suggest you build in enough to fund your required retirement or college education contribution. Should the unfortunate occur, spending patterns will no doubt change, but not as much as you would think, especially if there are children in the household.

The first step in this process is, of course, to decide how much life insurance you should have. The age-old financial planner's answer, *it depends*, applies more than ever here. In the old days, before computer modeling was readily available, life insurance agents would generalize that about five times current salary would be an appropriate amount. So start with that. But subjective factors, such as longevity, debts, age of children, investment assets levels and tax status would all come into play when arriving at the right amount.

It's interesting to note that the need for life insurance for lifestyle preservation usually peaks in your 30's and 40's if you have young children. As time goes on, into your 50's and 60's, the amount of life insurance needed to preserve future lifestyle generally reduces each year. This is why it's so important to review your coverage and strategies annually.

Following this logic, you would come to the conclusion that life insurance isn't much needed for those who are retired, whose children are grown and no longer depend on them for financial support. That could be accurate. In fact, at retirement age, by definition, we are no longer depending on income from work and therefore would not need income replacement from life insurance. In other words, life insurance for lifestyle preservation purposes becomes optional at that time. This, however, would generally not be true for people with large pensions that may not have some kind of survivor benefit.

It may seem counterintuitive to tell a younger person, when money is usually tight, that millions of dollars of life insurance is needed and that when they become more successful, when they probably can more easily afford it, they will need less.

The good news is that since the probability of death is lower when you are younger, so is the pure cost of life insurance. As you age, the risk of death increases and so does the cost of insurance, but you can partially offset this cost by reducing the coverage every few years. Be very careful how you apply this guideline, but it could help save you a lot of money in the long run.

Still, people in general are not yet comfortable with needing "millions of dollars of life insurance." Nonetheless, given the realities of today's lifestyle costs, especially for those for whom this book is written, you do need to get into the millions in coverage when it comes to adequate insurance levels. Once you have built your wealth and you have your own assets, you can consider self-insuring the risks, which simply means spending down your own resources.

Life Insurance can be confusing, so we'd like you to focus on the two major types. The first is "Term Insurance," which as the name implies covers you for a certain period of time, maybe 5, 10, 15 or 20 years. In order to collect on that policy, you need to die within that term period. If you buy a 10-year, $1 million policy, you'd have to cooperate and die within those ten years in order for your beneficiary to collect. Term is the less expensive type of insurance because you are only paying for the death benefit and not trying to build up a cash value.

The second is what is considered "Permanent or Whole Life" where the goal is to hold the policy until you are much older or until death. Typically this has a cash value attached to it that builds up, and will pay for the cost of insurance later in life, when insuring those later years would be more expensive.

This type of insurance, the permanent kind, starts out more expensive than term insurance, but in the long run, if you plan on having the insurance more than 15 to 20 years, you may find this to be a good investment. With these policies, you can also sometimes direct the type of investing the insurance company will do with your cash value each year. However, if you just want to make sure you 1) cover obligations over a certain amount of time, 2) keep your annual outlay low and 3) don't prioritize building up a future pool of cash, then term insurance may be your best bet.

Let's consider the couple who has three youngsters, who will all be in school for the next 15 years; they also have a mortgage with 25 years left on it. They want to make sure that if the husband dies prematurely, the family will still be able to meet its financial goals. He can simply buy a 25-year term insurance policy that would cover them if he dies during those 25 years. If he, hopefully, outlives the policy, he would then have no insurance, but since he bought the policy when he was younger he probably saved a lot on the premiums over the years. It's sort of like car insurance, where you are covered for a period of time, but when that time period is up, you have no cash value to it.

Term insurance is always cheaper in the short run. It may not be cheaper in the long run, but it may be a great option for those who have a tight cash flow today or better uses for their money.

Alternatively, if he had bought some kind of permanent policy, his payments would have been higher in the earlier years but a cash value would eventually build up which could be used to supplement long-term goals, such as college or even retirement. An insurance agent would be happy to explain the tax advantages of investing within an insurance policy, and there are some really good ones, but remember there are always fee structures to be considered and long-term surrender charges.

The topics you'll review during the summer season can be very emotional since it addresses important things in life—your family. Decisions made with regard to life insurance need to align with your overall estate plan and cash flow. This is specifically why we have brought these important topics together in one season.

Disability insurance if you become disabled and can't work

Unlike the risks of a premature death, the statistic on how many adults will suddenly be unable to earn a living is startling. According to the Social Security Administration, just over 1 in 4 of today's 20-year-olds will become disabled before the age of 67 due to health issues.

Disabilities are also almost impossible to anticipate. Over 90% are the result of an illness—a statistic based on research done by the Council on Disability Awareness. And it seems we are not preparing very well. While many of us rely on our employer for health insurance, only about 69% of employers in the private sector offer long-term disability insurance as part of their benefit packages. So that leaves you on your own to figure this one out. Should you buy a personal disability insurance policy? Should you elect your company's group benefits options? Depending on your age, this could be a very expensive type of coverage, but, in our opinion, it is one of the most important things to have. Here are some other thoughts to consider about disability insurance.

When considering purchasing a disability policy (also sometimes referred to as an income replacement policy) either on your own or from an employer's group plan, you need to carefully evaluate the insurance company's definition of being disabled. Find out if the disability insurance company will pay you if you can't perform the functions of your specific job, which is better and more expensive, or if you would only receive benefits if you could not perform any job. For instance, if you were an attorney and found yourself unable to perform the specific functions of an attorney, such as speaking clearly or clarity of thought and concepts, would your insurance company pay you? Or would they disqualify you if you could work in any other capacity, even "flipping burgers"?

Keep in mind that for most disability policies, companies will only pay you based on a percentage (rarely more than 65%) of your base salary—what that salary is at the time you apply for the insurance. It becomes critical to continually review your coverage as your income increases, or as a bonus or other alternative compensation becomes a bigger part of your earnings.

Lastly, here's a word about taxes on the proceeds from a disability policy. If you have personally paid the premiums to the disability insurance company, it is likely the monthly benefit you would receive would be tax-free. However, if your employer paid the premiums, the benefit might then be taxable to you. This is a big problem, because the amount you will receive is already discounted from what you normally make, and after paying taxes you might not have enough income to live on.

If you have the option to pay the premiums yourself with after-tax dollars through your employer, that might be the wiser choice. Also these policies will usually pay benefits only until you are 65, so as you get closer to that age, the benefit of having the coverage reduces.

Long Term Care – what is your strategy?

How many times have you heard stories about parents or loved ones who have reached a point in their lives where they can no longer fend for themselves? Family members, sons, daughters and spouses attempt to care for them, only to realize the overwhelming nature of attempting to feed, bath or dress a loved one day in and day out. Help is needed! Initially, this leads to interviewing adult care services that provide home care, only to realize the potential costs will only allow home care for a short period of time—not nearly enough to care for Mom or Dad! Emotions build, stress increases and the process of needing to move Mom or Dad to a nursing home has become a reality. However, can you afford to send Mom or Dad to the facility of their choosing? The answer, unfortunately for most, is no.

With the costs of most nursing homes well above one hundred thousand dollars annually, and the cost of proper home care similarly draining, most just cannot afford to pay for this care out of pocket. You may be doing fine, but what about your extended family? Most people in this situation, even if they initially can afford an acceptable level of care for their aging, disabled spouse or parents, find themselves potentially forced to spend every last dollar saved throughout their lifetime. The result is that most become impoverished and need to rely on the Medicaid system to care for the family member now residing in a nursing home—not the ideal scenario for anyone. However, with some simple planning earlier in life, many of these hard luck stories we hear can be averted.

This is where long-term care planning comes into play. This is the process of identifying whether or not a family can and/or should self-insure, utilizing their current resources to pay for home or nursing home care, or transfer the risk to an insurance company by investing in a long-term care policy. Most will not find it realistic to self-insure for the long haul, and therefore they need to consider including long-term care insurance as part of their future health care needs. Ideally, you want to begin to think about long-term care insurance in your forties, because the longer you wait the more expensive the coverage will be.

A long-term care policy will need to cover the daily activities of living, of which there are six. The six activities are as follows: bathing, dressing, eating, transferring, toileting and continence. An insurance provider will need to certify through a doctor that the policy owner is not able to conduct some or all of the activities of daily living in order to begin to collect on the policy. Most policies are offered in daily increments ($200, $300 per day care). How much you choose should be decided based on the resources you project to have during retirement, other income sources such as pensions and Social Security and where you plan on living during your retirement. It is important for the coverage to provide for both home and nursing home care. A waiting period is chosen; for most policies this can be up to 100 days. You'll also need to choose a length of coverage (perhaps 3 years, 5 years or even a lifetime benefit).

Policies can also have a cost of living adjustment rider of some sort to keep up with the rising cost of care. There are also unique features such as an international provision for care outside of the United States and even a tax benefit for those who qualify. A policy should be constructed based upon the needs of the individual being insured and the financial resources available to that person.

Long-term care is a part of financial planning that can no longer be an afterthought. It is a primary concern that needs to be reviewed annually.

Personal Umbrella Liability

It doesn't take a lawyer to recognize that our society has become increasingly litigious. Millions of civil lawsuits are filed in America every year. Frivolous or not, this fact is a potential threat to your family's resources and way of life. Are you effectively covered? Wait before you answer that, and don't think you're off the hook if your kids cause damage or injury to others; if they are living with you or driving your car, you can be liable.

Car insurance or home insurance will almost always have some level of liability coverage, but the liability limitations, many times, are too low for a major event. In actuality, the potential liability if someone is hurt in a major accident may well exceed millions of dollars, and most basic car and home policies fall well below that potential exposure. So please do an initial review now and add this to your summer mid-year activities. If you have less than $2 million or $3 million in liability coverage, you may want to consider adding an Umbrella or Excess Liability rider to your policy. For some people even $5 million might be more appropriate. It's not just what you own today that you need to protect but potentially your future income as well.

A good place to start would be your current car or home carrier who will know how to construct a base policy to fit the requirements of an Umbrella Policy. Don't worry: this is rarely a very costly policy and is well worth the money.

Intergenerational and Estate planning

Estate planning is the process intended to ensure that upon your death your investments and other belongings end up in the right hands, in the best way. If you plan properly, you can dictate just about any constraints that the recipients, also known as the beneficiaries, must follow to use or dispose of the assets. Basically, that means you can control which assets go to which beneficiaries, when they receive it, and even what the tax strategies will be. It also means you can dictate who does not end up sharing in your hard-earned wealth.

Estate planning begins with, well, *planning*. Think about it. Do you really trust your kids to make the right decisions? What about their spouses? Is it possible that their marriages might not work out and your assets might be exposed in a divorce? Perhaps you have no intention of giving assets to the son or daughter-in-law if the marriage does not survive.

Another thing to consider is what age is the right age for kids or grandkids to receive their inheritances, or should a trust be set up. Be careful not to leave money to a disabled child directly, as it may negatively impact aid programs.

What if some of your children have children and what if others do not—are you leaving the same amount to everyone? It's up to you to think this through.

What about charities? You need to clearly spell out bequests to charitable organizations, identifying the specific entities as well as the amounts. Actual amounts are also better than percentages.

When you are dealing with your home, it is probably best to clearly state in the Will what your wishes are; perhaps a directive to have it sold and distribute the proceeds. If you do not specifically state the plans for the ultimate disposition of the house, you can inadvertently put your children at odds with each other. You probably would want to avoid that if you can.

You should also consider who the perfect executor would be in the case of a Will, or the perfect Trustee in the event you set up a Trust. This person (or persons) will have all the responsibility (and liability) to make sure your instructions are followed. Certain Trusts should ideally be set up today to be most effective (i.e. Living or Inter-vivos Trusts). Sometimes a Trust is not needed until after death and the Will creates the Trust at death (i.e. a Testamentary Trust).

This whole area is one you most likely would be best served discussing with an experienced estate planning attorney. No estate planning can be accomplished without your first putting yourself through the challenging thought process that estate planning deserves. You need to be clear, not only about your current situation, but also about what the future could look like.

Regardless of how well the Will is contemplated today, we can assure you that your feelings and financial circumstances will change continuously, as will tax laws. Health situations and longevity issues always change, making it a must to do periodic reassessments of your estate and intergenerational planning.

Documents you should have

When developing an estate plan, one needs to be looking at and understanding the major types of documents that a family or individual need to have in place in case of an untimely death or a tragic accident where someone may be unconscious or otherwise unable to make decisions. What core documents should everyone have in place? Here are the three most common.

The Will

Basically the Will is a letter to the judge that says, "Hey, Your Honor, if you can't figure out what I wanted to do with my assets by any other written means, this letter, my Will, is what I would want." The critical thing to know is that the Will is not the first set of rules that will dictate what happens to your assets, but basically the last set of rules. The process that refers to transferring estate assets according to the Will is called probate. Sometimes probate is a valuable process and sometimes probate could have been avoided along with the legal costs, delays and stress involved. Probate assets are also general public knowledge that almost anyone can access.

Avoiding probate – what trumps the Will?

To alleviate the pain of your heirs from having to go through the arduous and costly probate process, where a judge needs to determine the distribution of your estate, there are many simple strategies you can use.

Accounts and assets that are in joint names or have a "transfer on death" instruction in the title of the account give a clear indication of who the account is intended for. Also, accounts that have beneficiaries, such as retirement plans and insurance policies, are usually non-probate items. With regard to beneficiaries, you should always set up a primary and then a backup—also known as a contingent beneficiary.

Most trusts do not go through the probate process, but this is a complicated area that your attorney should review with you. Sometimes it's best not to avoid the probate process and let the Will be the guide for certain assets and strategies. This is especially true if you have crafted more complex provisions such as Trusts. Assets intended to fund these trusts should be made to go through probate; otherwise you run the risk of having an unfunded or underfunded Trust, which is something we see a lot.

As far as the family home is concerned, it is common for this asset to be handled through the Will. That's probably best. To avoid this, you would have to rewrite the deed and incur other significant expenses, not to mention that doing this might be negatively viewed by your mortgage holder. Issues relating to the care of minor children would also be best handled through provisions in the Will.

Be careful with IRAs and other retirement accounts. These are usually best transferred through beneficiaries as opposed to through your Will. If not, you might inadvertently trigger a very large income tax bill much earlier than necessary.

When creating a Will, your thought process is usually more focused and comprehensive. Interestingly, this "document of last resort" is usually the one that gets the most thought. Many people do not put in the same effort when they fill out beneficiary forms for 401(k)s or even when they open a bank account. All this is important because right now, and for each and every annual review, you need to make certain there is no conflict, or what we call a *misalignment* in how all your estate documents treat your assets. You can download an estate planning organizer from our site at www.FinanciallySecureForever.com if you like.

A Will is a personal or individual document, and there is rarely a "family" Will. Each person, for example, husband and wife individually, must have their own Will. Part of the reason is that these documents give instructions only relating to that person's death. In the sad situation where people die together, the Will generally will make an assumption that one party has been deemed to have died first.

Power of Attorney and Health Care Directive
Two other documents are usually part of the basic estate planning portfolio. A Power of Attorney (a "Durable" POA is best

to have) and a Health Care Directive (or what is many times considered a Living Will, depending on your state of domicile). These are state-governed documents, so each state has its own sets of rules and forms.

As we've discussed before, we are not attorneys and our advice is for your general knowledge and planning. Everyone's situation is unique, so you need to think through each component carefully.

From our standpoint the Durable Power of Attorney is a most critical document to have. It is most often needed for times when someone is incapacitated. This document appoints an agent to manage your financial affairs (as opposed to health decisions) and is a protection for you when you are alive.

Having the right Power of Attorney in place will avoid problems if you need someone to access, sell or modify accounts that are in joint names. Without it, even though ownership may be jointly held, which will be relevant in case of death, incapacity of one of the owners can tie up the asset or assets for a very long time. You would not have the valid signatures needed to transfer a joint asset, such as a house or investment account, if one of the owners is not deemed competent. There are many other reasons to have a Durable Power of Attorney, but for it to be the most effective, it should be done proactively before anyone gets hurt or sick.

The Health Care Proxy or Living Will is similar to the Power of Attorney but is intended to appoint someone who can make serious, life-affecting medical decisions. These are decisions that may be difficult for anyone to make, so think carefully about who you want to appoint as your proxy. Few things are more personal than your wishes about the level of care and actions you want followed if you are in a critical care situation. It is a critical document that helps you establish clear instructions and clarifies your personal wishes.

As part of creating a Health Care Proxy, you'll need to choose an agent. The agent is the person you assign to make health care decisions for you. You need to think carefully about who knows you best, and who will be able to speak on your behalf regarding your health care matters. You should also consider where the person lives and whether that person could be present when health care decisions need to be made.

You should discuss your health care wishes with your proxy. You should also consider naming a second person in the event that your first choice is unavailable or unwilling to make the decisions.

Once you have signed the document, you should inform your physician and your family. If you change your mind after creating the document, you can amend or revoke it at any time.

Here are some scenarios to help you begin to think about intergenerational concepts. Granted, the first scenario is more normal, but the later scenario is not that far-fetched. It shows you how complicated it can get. Once you have thought through these situations, think about your own family structure. Start with a family tree and build from there. You will need to draw on this when you begin to work with your attorney.

First is the hypothetical couple who met in high school or college, have been happily married for forty years, with three grown children and four grandchildren. They have about $2 million, including their home, which is valued at about a half million dollars, and an IRA account with just over $1.2 million. They both were educators and have nice pensions. In fact, it's highly probable they will never need to tap into their nest egg for their own lifestyle, but they are generous to their kids, who have grown up in a very different financial world. One of their children, married with no kids, is doing exceptionally well financially but they are very concerned about the other two, who seem to be struggling. At the very least they thought it would be a good idea to offer to pay for college for the grandkids. After all, they could it afford it, right?

At a family gathering one day, the couple made an announcement, "It would be our pleasure to take care of all college costs for the grandchildren." They were happy to take this burden off the shoulders of their children, especially the struggling ones. After all, they thought, how much could it be? When they went to college, they paid about $500 per year for a good education. They had no idea it would be about $50,000 per year per child today. That's around an $800,000 expenditure for them in today's dollars, and still growing! They also didn't count on having to pay income taxes on all the IRA money. You can see how this one issue alone calls for an intergenerational approach.

Now let's look at another hypothetical couple, one that presents a very different dynamic. Let's call them a more "modern family." Both husband and wife have been divorced and each has two grown children. Two of their grown children have also been divorced and one is remarried. One of their four combined offspring is in an interracial marriage and has an adopted daughter from China. Another child, a son, is gay and has a partner to whom he has recently been married. That partner has children with a previous gay partner to whom he was once married, and he and his ex share custody of "the twins," who now have a relationship with this couple's gay son and his extended family.

Financially, some of these offspring are extremely successful; others are just barely making ends meet. Some of the members of this complex nuclear and extended family get along just fine, but there is inevitably also conflict among other members. This couple doing their estate planning can't stand one of their sons-in-law, and also differ from each other in some ways on how to divvy up their estate and who to trust with what. Plus, who are the recipients going to be on any insurance policies?

Factor in a possible large age difference between husband and wife, adult children who are jealous or resentful, an adult child who is wildly successful and needs less while another is not doing well and urgently needs (or down the road will need) a greater measure of parental support, and what you may have is a big bag of worms.

At this point aren't you happy you previously updated your Goal Tracking and Asset Allocation work from previous seasons? The summer's Family Security and Cash Flow planning requires very different thought processes and emotions.

Next we move on to one of the most stressful topics on which successful people need to focus: the need to have an organized tax planning approach.

"Let our advance worrying become advance thinking and planning."

"The best way to predict the future is to invent it."

Chapter 7

Year-End Tax Planning Season: Fall

TIME FOR YOUR IDEAL SCENARIO, NO SURPRISES

I T'S NOT THAT much fun to write about taxes. It's probably even less fun for you to read about them, but as Benjamin Franklin famously noted, the issue is certainly not going to go away.

This chapter will help you make dynamic tax planning decisions. It will also help put you and your tax preparer on the same page early enough to proactively develop and manage your tax decisions for the year. You'll find it extremely helpful that we've dedicated the entire last season of the year to Tax Planning.

Since we assume the reader of this book is somewhat experienced already, we will forego the basics. For some, this will be a refresher on your strategies; for others, it may be an opportunity to implement new ones. Regardless, we want to make sure that you have the information you will need that can help you to eventually save on taxes, either for the current year or perhaps for some time in the future. This is information that can also assist you with questions you can discuss with your tax professionals.

We have intentionally tried to simplify and generalize here to make our points, and we strongly recommend that you contact your tax professional for a more detailed analysis of your specific situation. That said, our point is that your tax experts need adequate time, clarity and structure to give you their best advice. A lack of structured planning most definitely results in unnecessary taxes and, to make it worse, unnecessary penalties. So who is to blame if you make the wrong decisions? The answer has to be that *you* are, until you transfer some of that responsibility to another professional. But remember that you are really just transferring the work. You are the person who will pay the government if it's not done right. You need to take charge of this process. This chapter will begin to show you how.

First, carve out time for year-end tax planning. Remember, we have intentionally designed the previous three Seasons of Advice® segments to cover every other category of your required financial planning, so now you can exclusively focus this last Season of the year on taxes. Spend your time wisely and don't worry about spending too much energy on investments, insurance or even cash flow. If you've followed our model, these should be under control at this point. Before you know it, the new Goal Tracking Season will be here and you will start the process all over again so you will always remain current and informed about your financial picture and at the helm of *You Inc*.

At the end of this chapter, we provide a list of questions and activities you can follow to get organized and be able to conduct a productive pre-year-end tax planning conversation with your tax professional. We have also created a checklist you can use to prepare a summary to make both your time and your accountant's time productive. The checklist will try to bring up some trigger concepts that can shed light on tax saving opportunities. You can download an electronic copy with our compliments at **www.Financially-Secure-Forever.com**.

Let's begin with some broad concepts you should be aware of that are "tax relevant" for more successful people like you.

First, you need to understand that traditional tax planning is usually about either delaying taxable income or accelerating deductions but both require a good guess as to where the tax rates are headed. However, in this era of uncertainty about tax rates, you need to be careful. As we've said before, you are highly encouraged to use your professionals to help you think through these issues.

To illustrate the point that it's foolish to predict tax rates over the long term, just look at the historical top marginal tax rates over the years. The top marginal federal rate has ranged from 92% down to 28%.

Historical Highest Marginal Income Tax Rates

Year	Top Marginal Rate	Year	Top Marginal Rate	Year	Top Marginal Rate
1913	7.0%	1947	86.45%	1981	69.13%
1914	7.0%	1948	82.13%	1982	50.00%
1915	7.0%	1949	82.13%	1983	50.00%
1916	15.0%	1950	91.00%	1984	50.00%
1917	67.0%	1951	91.00%	1985	50.00%
1918	77.0%	1952	92.00%	1986	50.00%
1919	73.0%	1953	92.00%	1987	38.50%
1920	73.0%	1954	91.00%	1988	28.00%
1921	73.0%	1955	91.00%	1989	28.00%
1922	56.0%	1956	91.00%	1990	31.00%
1923	58.0%	1957	91.00%	1991	31.00%
1924	46.0%	1958	91.00%	1992	31.00%
1925	25.0%	1959	91.00%	1993	39.60%
1926	25.0%	1960	91.00%	1994	39.60%
1927	25.0%	1961	91.00%	1995	39.60%
1928	25.0%	1962	91.00%	1996	39.60%
1929	24.0%	1963	91.00%	1997	39.60%
1930	25.0%	1964	77.00%	1998	39.60%
1931	25.0%	1965	70.00%	1999	39.60%
1932	63.0%	1966	70.00%	2000	39.60%
1933	63.0%	1967	70.00%	2001	38.60%
1934	63.0%	1968	75.25%	2002	38.60%
1935	63.0%	1969	77.00%	2003	35.00%
1936	79.0%	1970	71.75%	2004	35.00%
1937	79.0%	1971	70.00%	2005	35.00%
1938	79.0%	1972	70.00%	2006	35.00%
1939	79.0%	1973	70.00%	2007	35.00%
1940	81.10%	1974	70.00%	2008	35.00%
1941	81.00%	1975	70.00%	2009	35.00%
1942	88.00%	1976	70.00%	2010	35.00%
1943	88.00%	1977	70.00%	2011	35.00%
1944	94.00%	1978	70.00%	2012	35.00%
1945	94.00%	1979	70.00%		
1946	86.45%	1980	70.00%		

Note: This table contains a number of simplifications and ignores a number of factors, such as a maximum tax on earned income of 50 percent when the top rate was 70 percent and the current increase in rates due to income-related reductions in value of itemized deductions. Perhaps most importantly, it ignores the large increase in percentage of returns that were subject to this top rate.

Sources: Eugene Steuerle, The Urban Institute; Joseph Pechman, Federal Tax Policy; Joint Committee on Taxation, Summary of Conference Agreement on the Jobs and Growth Tax Relief Reconciliation Act of 2003, JCX-54-03, May 22, 2003; IRS Revised Tax Rate Schedules

Do you really think anyone can tell you definitively what the future will bring with regard to tax rates? It is the repetitive process of the Seasonal cycle that will help you make the right strategic tax decisions.

Long-Term Capital Gains, 1977–2007 (2)

Year	Realized Long-Term Capital Gains	Taxes Paid on Long-Term Capital Gains	Average Effective Tax Rate (percent)	Maximum Tax Rate on Long-Term Gains
1977	43,755	7,870	18.0	39.875
1979	70,493	10,405	14.8	28.00
1980	69,856	10,817	15.5	28.00
1981	77,071	11,934	15.5	28.00/20.00
1982	86,087	12,500	14.5	20.00
1983	116,015	17,134	14.8	20.00
1984	135,936	20,365	15.0	20.00
1985	166,356	25,178	15.1	20.00
1986	318,944	50,834	15.9	20.00
1987	140,386	31,791	22.6	28.00
1988	153,271	36,746	24.0	28.00
1989	141,069	32,351	22.9	28.00
1990	115,671	25,900	22.4	28.00
1991	98,363	21,581	21.9	28.93
1992	114,060	25,847	22.7	28.93
1993	134,469	31,393	23.3	29.19
1994	140,392	33,092	23.6	29.19
1995	158,955	38,368	24.1	29.19
1996	233,872	58,782	25.1	29.19
1997	330,360	69,572	21.1	29.19/21.19
1998	424,762	80,611	19.0	21.19
1999	482,181	91,416	19.0	21.19
2000	588,061	111,507	19.0	21.19
2001	322,831	58,750	18.2	21.17
2002	251,301	44,984	17.9	21.16
2003	294,811	44,903	15.2	21.05/16.05
2004	466,224	66,154	14.2	16.05
2005	648,430	92,304	14.2	16.05
2006	750,771	106,568	14.2	15.70
2007 (3)	861,220	121,933	14.2	15.70

(1) Data include returns with positive total net capital gains, both short and long-term.
(2) Data include returns with positive long-term gains in excess of any short-term losses.
(3) Preliminary estimate, subject to revision.
Notes: Data include returns with positive long-term gains in excess of any short-term losses. Data for each year include some prior year tax returns. The maximum rate is the effective rate applying to high-income taxpayers, including the effects of provisions that alter effective rates for significant amounts of gains. Maximum rates include the effects of exclusions (1954-86), alternative tax rates (1954-86,1991-97), the minimum tax (1970-78), the alterna ive minimum tax (1979-), income tax surcharges (1968-70), and the phaseout of itemized deductions (3% 1991-2005, 2% 2006-07). The maximum statutory rate on long-term gains was 28% starting 1991, 20% starting May 1997 and 15% starting May 2003. Since 1997, gains on collectibles and certain deprecia ion recapture are taxed at ordinary rates, up to maximum rates of 28% on collectibles and 25% on recapture. Midyear rate changes occurred in 1978, 1981, 1997 and 2003. Estimates are subject to revision.
Source: Department of the Treasury, Office of Tax Analysis (December 30, 2010 and January 14, 2010).

One place where this is very relevant is the ubiquitous choice of deferring income to fund retirement plans, presuming rates will be lower in retirement. Will they? Perhaps, but if you guess wrong you may have made a huge mistake—especially when you realize that retirement plan withdrawals are currently taxed at the higher ordinary income tax rates—basically the highest rates we pay. However, if you elected not to defer your income, yes, you would have to pay ordinary rates on the income today, but all the future earnings on this money could possibly be paid at the lower capital gains rates, or even less if you use a ROTH IRA.

Sure, you would lose the current deduction; but in the long run, you may end up with more money. Look at the history of Long Term Capital Gains Rates from 1977–2007.

You need to take some time to try to get this all figured out. Clear the decks, focus your mind, and think the issues through. Also keep in mind that tax laws change unpredictably almost every year, and sometimes even more frequently than that. A college tax instructor once said that the biggest mistake people make is to assume that tax laws make sense when in fact they are simply the result of a negotiation between political parties. Don't always assume a logical foundation to what the tax code allows you to do or not do. Then, once the law is in place, it may be inconsistently applied by the IRS or other authorities. They have limitations too. In addition there are unique situations that are occasionally proposed and agreed to in Private Letter Rulings from the IRS to individual taxpayers. This can also affect the way the tax law is applied, as do the rulings and opinions of the various tax courts. Finally (and of course not really finally), is the fact that most tax laws hit each of us differently depending on our socioeconomic situation, number of dependents, deductions, etc. Did you know there is also an "Alternative Minimum Tax" rate schedule to deal with? We'll discuss more about that later.

It should be crystal clear to you right now that installing a structured Tax Planning Season into your financial year makes sense. Again, this is why you should always have excellent professional tax advisors. It gets pretty complicated for someone who doesn't have a "feel" for these things.

So let's begin our Tax Planning Season. As we said, the objective ultimately is to be able to have a pre-year-end tax-planning meeting with your accountant and it's probably best to schedule this between October 15th and Thanksgiving—generally an available time for accountants. This timing will also give both you and your accountant adequate time to absorb the issues and implement your decisions before the arrival of the New Year.

Start gathering the information for your tax planning meeting

Before meeting with the professional, give yourself enough time to accumulate relevant information. If you are an employee working for a company, you will need your most recent paycheck information or online version thereof. Your most up-to-date broker's statement and record of estimated taxes paid, if any, will also be necessary.

To be practical, we'll mostly stay with a discussion of federal taxes in this chapter. State taxes are usually similar but will always have unique nuances that your tax advisor can highlight for you.

Here are ten commonly overlooked areas we see when we deal with smart and successful individuals like you.

1. **Overpaying estimated and withholding taxes**
   Accountants deserve great credit for helping you get refunds, but financial planners prefer that you break even, having been able to use all your money during the year to meet your other financial goals. In the end, of course, the IRS will settle up with you, but by then you're probably already overpaid for the next year.

A common question is whether or not to pay quarterly estimated taxes. For most employees withholding is close enough. However, when unusual circumstances lead to an underpayment in the previous year, the accountant's software will recommend (and the IRS guidelines suggest) quarterly estimated payments for the next year. However, many times the unusual circumstances that caused the underpayment in the previous year may not exist in future years. So why then would you send extra money to the government when you don't need to? Of course, you wouldn't—or shouldn't—if that turns out to be the case. If you suspect you're paying more estimated taxes than you will need, it's okay to adjust or even eliminate your remaining estimated tax payments.

The Tax Planning Season should determine if you are in good shape with your tax deposits. Do you even need to make the last January 15th payment? With earlier detection you might even have been able to skip the earlier September 15th and June 15th payments.

Be aware that most payroll systems do not adjust your taxable income for the 401(k) contributions you are making. These contributions defer the income out of the current year, so there are no current taxes due on this amount. This sometimes results in over-withholding. With professional guidance, consider adjusting your exemptions to get to a more accurate tax liability.

2. **Underpaying estimated and withholding taxes and incurring penalties**
The federal government expects you to pay as you earn. If you are an employee, the withholding charts are a guideline, but there is no guarantee you will not need to pay more.

Higher earners, as you probably know, are expected to have paid in at least 90% of the current tax bill before January 15th following the end of the tax year, or at least 100% of the previous year's actual tax. This is what we call the "protect approach."

For many people the standard tax deduction tables will provide adequate withholding protection. However, as you move up the ladder, unique situations may cause an underpayment. For people with bonuses, stock options, etc. many companies opt for a standard statutory withholding rate. This could, in fact, be less than your actual liability, so be aware. Also watch out for potential inherited IRAs and annuities.

Perhaps you received outside income from somewhere this year and no taxes whatsoever were taken out. This is very common if you have significant investment transactions, consulting income, business interests, pensions, social security or even unemployment income. This is often overlooked until it's too late.

We have also repeatedly seen underpayment occur when both spouses work but one has a much lower income than the other. Although the lesser income earner will have the proper taxes withheld based on the individual required tables, this standardized formula rarely reflects the marginal tax rates when the income of *both* spouses are taken together. (Yes, even if "married" is claimed).

3. Inappropriate cost basis on sales of individual stocks and bonds

Failing to keep good records will almost always result in your overpaying taxes when dealing with an investment portfolio. You have choices about when and how much tax you will pay on stock and bond sales. For practical purposes, in this book we'll keep it simple.

Specific Identification vs. Average Cost vs. FIFO vs. LIFO
Let's say you bought 100 shares of XYZ stock in 1997
at a price of $50. Then you bought another 100 shares
in 2007 at $100, and more recently you bought another
100 shares at $150 per share. So you now own 300
shares of XYZ with a total cost of $30,000. XYZ is now
selling for $120 per share and you decide to sell half of
your holdings or 150 shares, resulting in sales proceeds
of $18,000. What is your profit for tax purposes?

a) Loss of $2,000 (LIFO method[1])

b) Gain of $8,000 (FIFO method[2])

c) Gain of $3,000 (Average cost method[3])

d) None (Specific identification method[4])

Answer: They all could be correct, depending on the
method you choose. The IRS gives you a choice to
determine your method but the deal is that whatever
method you choose, you must be consistent for that
stock going forward. In the long run, you will recognize all the profit, but you and your tax advisors have a
choice as to what best fits your situation.

---

[1] Under LIFO (Last-in First-out) the 150 shares sold are deemed to have come from the
100 last shares purchased at $150 or $15,000, plus 50 shares from the 2nd grouping
at $100 each for another $5,000. The total cost basis for tax purposes would then be
$20,000 under the LIFO method, resulting in a $2,000 loss.

[2] Under FIFO (First-in First-out) the 150 shares sold are deemed to have come from the
original 100 shares purchased at $50 or $5,000, plus 50 shares from the 2nd grouping at
$100 for another $5,000. The total cost basis for tax purposes under the FIFO method
then would be $10,000, resulting in a gain of $8,000.

[3] Under the Average Cost method, the 300 shares cost a total of $30,000 or $100 per
share. The sale of 150 shares at $120 results in a $20 per share profit or a gain of $3,000.

[4] Under the Specific Identification method, you choose which shares you are selling. It is
possible to say that you had *no gain* on this sale at all because we sold 25 shares from
first group ($1,250 cost), 70 shares from the 2nd group ($7,000 cost), and 65 shares
from the 3rd group ($9,750 cost) for a total cost of $18,000. Clearly it is important that
you keep excellent records here.

By the way, if you fail to tell your broker which method you choose, they will report to the IRS based on the FIFO method.

Watch your holding period

Be well aware of where you are with respect to long-term versus short-term capital gain treatment. Sometimes it makes sense to wait until you have one year under your belt before selling so that you can benefit from the better long-term rates. But, of course, we don't suggest this to be the only consideration.

Harvest Tax Losses

Even if your portfolio is doing well overall, it may make sense for you to sell the losers and use those losses to offset your gains for the year. You can also offset your ordinary income by as much as $3,000 or store those losses for future use. Short-term losses are more valuable, especially if you have short-term gains. This is a complicated area requiring consultation with your accounting and tax specialists. This is yet another reason to carve out time for Tax Planning.

4. Watch out for year-end surprises from mutual funds

So you've chosen to use mutual funds to help implement your investment plan? That's a smart decision. The diversification that mutual funds provide is hard to beat. But there are tax "gotcha's" to watch out for.

To begin, mutual funds are required to distribute their profits each year, and they do so in the form of capital gain distributions that generally occur near the end of the year. The earnings come from stocks sold in the current year, but the actual appreciation before selling could have accumulated over time, even before you became a shareholder.

The fact that you weren't around to reap the rewards the whole time the fund was making the money doesn't matter to the IRS. In a strategy similar to musical chairs, whoever is holding the mutual fund share at the time the music stops, or the distribution is declared, pays taxes on the income on the *entire* amount, even if the investor only held that mutual fund for less than a year, even one day, and even if your personal position was at a loss at the time.

The lesson here is, don't buy mutual funds that pay capital gains later in the year unless you are aware of the tax risk and still love the investment anyway. This is a common rookie mistake that even professional financial advisors have occasionally made as well. You can wait until the day after the distribution is paid and you will be in a better tax position.

Don't pay the same taxes twice

There are some other things to watch out for when it comes to mutual funds. Unlike the individual securities described previously, you'll probably want to go with the average cost basis reported to you by the mutual fund company. If you do not, and you can remember you paid $X for the fund and now 3 years later you sold it for $Y and your profit was $Z, you still want to be careful. It is possible that over the years you already paid taxes on the capital gains during the years. You are entitled to deduct those previously reported gains against your overall profit. *Make sure you don't pay them twice!* The average price method adjusts for this and it's best to take that from the investment firm's 1099 form.

5. **Missing deductions and credits that don't appear on tax forms**

Simply put, there are items that are tax relevant that don't show up on annual tax information forms like W-2's or 1099's. To save time, we won't list them here.

Instead, we'll provide some items to look for in the checklist at the end of this chapter and also online at **www.Financially-Secure-Forever.com**. This will help prepare you for your year-end tax meeting with your accountant.

We urge you to take time and be thorough in your process. Remember things like investment advice fees, long-term care insurance premiums, and donations to certain educational accounts are items that may be deductible. Even the fact that you refinanced or purchased a new home is a valuable piece of information often not reported to the accountant or IRS.

6. Personal retirement plans can shelter extra income

If you are one of the lucky ones who earn extra income on the side, no matter how much, you may have opportunities to save on taxes.

If you are not an employee of the firm that paid you, you have become, in effect, a small business owner. Outside income is usually reported on Schedules C or E of your tax return. If this applies to you, the IRS says you may write off some of this income by creating a separate retirement program just for this outside income.

It could be a SEP-IRA (Simplified Employee Pension Individual Retirement Arrangement) which is the most common, but it could also be a more complicated and substantial, plan such as a defined benefit plan, where you could write off as much as half of the income or more.

There are complicated decisions that may require you to gather and evaluate your options and, in some cases, involve paperwork that needs to be completed by December 31st.

7. Ignorance of the Alternative Minimum Tax

One of the most frustrating things you'll probably deal with in the tax arena is something called the Alternative

Minimum Tax (AMT). Some people are subject to it and some are not. For many successful people, the AMT is a common occurrence.

Suddenly, things like real estate taxes, state income taxes and other deductions that are bedrock deductions become severely diluted or eliminated entirely within the AMT calculation. This is a shock to most people.

Is this fair? We're not here to argue, but you should understand that before the AMT, it was not uncommon to see headlines about the very rich who found ways to write off all their income. At first, the AMT was a way to say that write-offs shouldn't represent too high a percentage of income. It was originally intended as a way to reduce excessive deductions for the extremely wealthy.

However, that was in 1969. Today, with just normal inflation and cost of living, more and more "regular" people are falling into this alternative calculation. Today it affects millions of taxpayers. You need to know where you stand.

If you are in AMT-ville, watch out! Some of your tax-exempt bonds may actually be taxable; some of the gains on stocks that you thought were falling under the favored long-term capital gains rates actually will not be counted that way. If you are not in the AMT this year but might be next year, or vice versa, you might want to consider accelerating or delaying potential deductions.

The IRS form 6251 is a worksheet for the Alternative Minimum Tax and should be attached to your return. If you are not sure if you are exposed to the AMT, just look at page 2 of your IRS tax form 1040 and you will see a line where AMT taxes are entered. If there is a number on that line, you're in it, and let the planning begin with your tax professional.

If you do your own return, or just don't want to ask your accountant, the IRS provides an AMT Assistant questionnaire that can be found on their website at **www.IRS.gov**

8. Failing to consider ROTH accounts in retirement planning

ROTH IRA accounts have been around since 1998. However, it seems like the public and their employers are just getting around to understanding the incredible power of this retirement tool. In short, we love them, but you need to know the rules, and your tax advisor should be your first stop.

In a ROTH IRA scenario, you experience the reverse of what would happen in a traditional retirement account. Instead of deferring income tax today in favor of paying tomorrow, the ROTH IRA says go ahead and pay tax today and then in the future *everything*, including the current contribution and earnings from day one, are tax-free. This can be an enormous planning tool.

If you like the concept of the ROTH IRA, you may also be able to convert your existing Traditional IRA accounts to ROTH IRAs. You might be able to establish new accounts and your company may have created a ROTH 401(k) option for you to consider. You need to know more about these if your company has added that feature to your plan. Many have and, for some reason, employees are unaware.

ROTH IRAs have unique attributes that may be valuable for home buyers, education funding, estate planning and much more. It can significantly change tax rates on eventual retirement plan distributions and become an excellent long-term planning tool to keep marginal rates down in the future.

9. Improper handling of company stock in old 401(k) plans

A little known rule exists regarding highly appreciated company stock that is in a 401(k) plan. When an employee leaves the company, there is the option for him or her to pay the tax at regular ordinary income rates (high) on the cost basis of when that stock was first put into the plan, which might be much lower than current values. The company will provide this cost basis. The difference, which could be substantial, would then be subject to capital gains rates (lower) when it is eventually sold, short or long term depending on how long it's held. If you are over 55, it's best if you opt to do this.

While it's painful to pay tax earlier than you would need to, the ability to convert the earnings retroactively to capital gains rates is a substantial benefit. The strategy is called Net Unrealized Appreciation (NUA). Many investment brokers hate it because it reduces the assets they manage in the short term and therefore the fees they earn. If you have company stock in your 401(k), make sure the NUA strategy is considered before you roll anything over to an IRA or new company plan.

The alternative scenario would be to just sell off the company stock and invest the whole amount without paying any taxes until the eventual distribution. However, as we've mentioned, those distributions are subject to usually higher tax rates.

As with any tax planning strategy, the answer is: It depends on your circumstances, when you will withdraw the funds, etc.

10. Mixing personal and business expenses together

If you have legitimate business expenses, you should deduct them. People have asked us if certain expenses increase the chance of an audit, and they do. However, if you have a legitimate deductible expense, by all means, go ahead. Always make sure you have a structured way of isolating those expenses and not comingling them with personal expenses. The IRS doesn't like that and, quite frankly, we don't either.

In this case, form is just as important as substance, especially if your deductions are ever questioned under audit. You must have a good system, with logs, for multiuse items, such as cars or telephones. As for the most frequently asked item? We direct any questions with regard to home office expenses to your accountant, who can explain the complex rules and the effects of depreciation and recapture to you.

If you comingle expenses, there is always the likelihood you may entirely forget that you had that deduction and what the correct amount was.

If you do have ongoing business expenses, consider creating a separate bank account. You do not need to have a separate corporation to open a separate bank account. Ask your banker. On the other hand, many people have chosen to become their own bookkeepers and now use accounting software to track expenses. That's nice perhaps, but you may end up taking on extra work that could just as easily been done manually.

If you determine that you have legitimate business expenses, you basically have two options for where to deduct these on your tax return. Schedule A allows you to deduct unreimbursed business expenses as a miscellaneous item, subject to a 2% of adjusted gross income (AGI) limitation. If you are in AMT or have a large enough income where your deductions are curtailed, you will get a better bang for the deduction on Schedule C or E, if it applies to your situation. Again, make this a priority conversation item with your accountant during your Tax Planning Season.

In Summary

Successful people do tax planning in advance each year. Carving out the last season of the year for taxes will improve your personal tax system for today and for many more tomorrows.

To further help you think through some issues before your tax planning meeting with the accountant, we have prepared the following checklist. There are a many questions but it really shouldn't take you much more than an hour to fill it out. To jog your memory, keep a running log of tax-related items and questions that come up during the year.

The Tax Planning Season will help you manage the inherent stress this subject invites each year. The Seasons of Advice process will help you create your agenda when meeting with your accountant before year end. An electronic copy of this checklist can be found on our website at **www.Financially-Secure-Forever.com.**

Now you can see why we wanted you to take care of all the other issues in previous seasons.

Good Luck!

Tax Planning Agenda Worksheet

Here are our top 50 items we think your tax preparer might want to know:

Taxpayer name(s):

Age(s):

Previous Year's Filing Status:

Current Year's Anticipated Filing Status:

1. Do you own a business, either directly or indirectly? If so, how much is the net expected income from this business this year?

2. Does your return include a K-1?

3. Did you receive unemployment compensation during the year?

4. Did you receive Social Security benefits?

5. Adjusted gross income on last year's tax return $ _____

   Anticipated for current year $ _____

   Anticipated income for next year $ _____

6. Are you paying quarterly estimated taxes?

7. Do you have a desire to make current charitable contributions? If yes,

   Charitable contributions shown
   on last year's return $ _____

   Anticipated charitable contributions
   for current year $ _____

   Anticipated charitable contributions
   income for next year $ _____

   Has any previous charitable deduction been limited because of the AGI rules?

8. Did you pay the Alternative Minimum Tax last year?

   Do you expect to pay AMT this year?

9. What is the amount of your tax refund/tax due arising from last year's return?

10. Do you own municipal bonds?

11. Are you investing in a tax-exempt mutual fund? If yes, contact the fund company or go on its website to determine which part of the dividend/interest is subjected to the federal AMT and/or individual state and local taxes.

12. Do you have any unused capital loss carryovers?

13. Do you have investment accounts?

    Est. Realized Gains   Est. Realized Losses
    Short term   Long term
    $ _____ $ _____

    Est. Unrealized Gains   Est. Unrealized Losses
    Short term   Long term
    $ _____ $ _____

14. Has previous capital gain distributions from mutual funds been taken into consideration when calculating capital gains?

15. Did you redeem any U.S. Savings Bonds?

16. Has your marital status changed?

17. Did you add or subtract exemptions this year?

18. Are you paying for more than half the support of another individual?

19. Are you saving for education? If so, how much per child?

    Has a 529 plan been used? If yes, what state? (Note, there are different income state benefits depending on the state's particular plan.)

20. Do you have children under 18 (19-23 for full-term students)?

21. Did you make gifts of over $13,000 to an individual?

    Did you make gifts appreciated securities?

22. Have you paid any tuition?

23. Have you paid any student loan interest?

24. Are you funding a SIMPLE IRA, SEP IRA, 401(k), 403(b), Profit Sharing,

    Money Purchase, Defined Benefit Plan or Roth 401(k)?

    Have you made any contributions for this year?

25. Did you make any Roth IRA conversions this year?

    Do you qualify?

26. Have you ever converted a traditional IRA to Roth IRA?

27. Do you qualify for a traditional IRA contribution?

28. Will you make a non-deductible IRA contribution?

29. Can you qualify for Roth IRA contributions? If so, how much will you contribute?

30. Did you roll over your previous employer's pension into your IRA?

31. Are you over the age of 59 ½?

32. Have any pension or retirement plan distributions been made?

33. Are you over the age of 70 ½? How much required minimum distribution will you need to take this year?

34. Do you have any incentive stock options? If yes, have any Incentive Stock Options been exercised during the year?

35. Do you have any Non-Qualified Stock Options? Have you exercised any of them this year?

36. Do you have Restricted Stock Award?

    Have you made a Section 83b Election?

    How much was paid out this year?

37. Do you participate in a company deferred compensation program?

38. Do you take advantage of an employer's flex spending plans ?

    If yes, how much? Has it all been used this year?

39. Did you buy/sell a home this year?

    If so, please provide details (profit, cost basis, mortgage, etc.)

40. Do you own investment real estate or investment real estate trust?

41. Have you refinanced this year? Has the client previously refinanced?

42. Were there extensive medical and dental expenses, casualty losses, unreimbursed business expenses or job seeking costs?

43. Has any of your family members passed away in last year? If yes, should an alternate estate valuation be considered?

44. Has margin interest been paid this year? If so, has the proceeds been used for purposes other than taxable investments?

45. Do you participate in a Health Savings Account?

46. Did you receive any COBRA benefits this year?

47. Did you surrender or terminate any insurance policies or annuities?

48. Are you paying for Long Term Care insurance? If so, how much is the premium?

49. Did you install energy saving devices (such as adding insulation, energy efficient exterior windows and energy-efficient heating and air conditioning systems)?

50. Did you adopt a child this year?

"*Unless commitment is made, there are only promises and hopes... but no plans.*"

PETER DRUCKER, business expert (1909–2005)

"*A man is not old until his regrets take the place of dreams.*"

YIDDISH PROVERB

Chapter 8

Retirement

ARE YOU PLANNING to retire? If so, have you given serious thought to how and when? Most of all, do you know what you want to be doing in your retirement? Whatever that is, will you be able to afford it? Are you ready to make choices?

The first big question is: Do you really want to retire—as in do no meaningful work for pay ever again, and if you plan to work on a volunteer basis, is it okay with you if you make no more money? We ask because even people who don't necessarily need more money still find being well paid for what they do a fun scorecard of how the world perceives their contribution.

Today 70 is the new 50, as some would have it. More than 30 years ago, Gloria Steinem, when asked how she looked so youthful, she famously replied, "This is what 40 looks like." Gloria is still writing her bestsellers, traveling globally for vital humanitarian causes, and generally still living with the same zeal, commitment, enthusiasm and energy she had at 40. This is now becoming more of the role model most of us aspire to than the image of a wrinkled granny or gramps on the porch in a rocking chair, false teeth resting in a glass in the bathroom.

If you factor in how long human beings have been around, retirement is actually a relatively new concept. It was first introduced during the 19th and 20th centuries. Previously, much lower life expectancy and the absence of pensions meant that most people would continue to work until their deaths; perhaps, in earlier days, that meant on the farm or in the factory. Nowadays most developed countries have systems to provide retirement pensions, which may be sponsored by employers or the state.

Of course, your personal lifestyle, your habits, how you live now and will want to live in that stage of your life has much to do with being able to retire. Or, to be more accurate, whether being able to retire in *style* is real for you, or just a mirage. Interestingly, retirement is not nearly as much about money as most people think. Imagine you bought a winning lottery ticket and have just won $50 million, or a million dollars each year for life. Even after taxes that's quite a payout. How would unlimited funds change your life? Think about it. It's a good exercise because it will give you insights into your own subconscious makeup.

Statistically, according to several reliable polls, most people who experience a windfall make far less changes in their lifestyle than you might think. The thrifty are still thrifty; the spendthrift still blows right through it.

This main finding in surveys and polls is no surprise to us because we see it all the time with our clients: a majority insist that when they reach retirement age, they prefer to continue to do some kind of work instead of going on what one might consider a permanent vacation. Retirement may more often mean that people want the freedom to choose their work, to volunteer more, or to switch to a less lucrative pursuit.

For others, addressing retirement is the trigger to uncovering concerns about having their livelihood protected in case of emergencies, such as failing health, being fired, or the sudden need to care for an aging parent. We find that regardless of individual ideas about retirement, the underlying goal for everyone centers around reaching a point of reasonable security, and having freedom of choice in the event of a financial downturn.

In truth, it's not always easy to be certain that the type of retirement you want is the type of retirement you get. Naturally the majority of people try their best to plan ahead intelligently. So how can you help insure your ideal retirement is going to be a reality rather than an unattainable mirage? Will your plan bear fruit when you are ready? Are you prepared enough if, for unexpected reasons, it comes sooner than you think?

Your retirement security is a vital area, and one in which the Seasons of Advice approach can be extremely valuable. To begin to understand how this may apply to your situation, let's look at two very different clients. These are people with similar incomes and goals but different overall net worth and a vastly differing ability to achieve their dreams.

Maxine and Andrew

The first couple, who we'll call Maxine and Andrew, a British couple here in the U.S., came to us late in their financial life. Both were in their mid-fifties. They were referred by friends of theirs we had helped to retire early, and Andrew's goal was to do the same. He was a highly-sought-after engineer who often consulted in several Arab republics. He'd just been offered early retirement and was eager to do so. The couple were keen for him to travel less and be home more, partly to enjoy their mutual passion for growing new varieties of roses. In retirement, Andrew planned to continue bringing in income through his real estate investments.

With that in mind, we went through their portfolio and personal finances in great detail. Regretfully, we did not have such good news for them. Their investments were primarily in high-end real estate in markets that were experiencing significant downturns. They paid high dollars for impressive but less commercial properties and built lush gardens on them "to improve the investment." The expenses and maintenance on these beautiful but less practical investment properties created an extremely high overhead for them. You might say that it was their passion for roses, not their business sense, that was leading their investing strategy.

In addition, both Andrew and Maxine were spenders. Over time, they had highly leveraged most of the properties to support their second home, their investment properties, the gardens and their overall lavish lifestyle.

Immersed in his successful consultancy, Andrew was out of the country much of the year. He was busy and distracted from the kind of connection to his financial planning that would ensure the retirement they both assumed for themselves. As we spoke, they both became very concerned, if not dismayed, to learn their debt structure and the current marketplace not only made immediate retirement unthinkable but threatened to sink their ship entirely.

As we reviewed their past spending, they saw with shock that they had actually been insolvent for some time. Andrew did make a great deal of money each year, but they also spent his entire earnings on their luxurious, jet-setter life. In fact, their situation needed urgent attention or they would be in grave crisis. If they were to preserve anything, they would have to begin immediately to alter their lifestyle by selling properties, as well as making other adjustments, all of which added up to less spending.

Maxine and Andrew had an unpleasant wakeup call, but sometimes a wakeup call is just what's needed. Fortunately, that was the case with them. We first had them create new goals and dreams—ones within reach in their current financial picture. These required tough choices: if they could possibly save one of their two homes, the main home or the retreat, which one should it be? Which one of their ten "investment" properties would they keep? Was Maxine, who worked only sporadically, willing to return to work as an educational consultant?

Armed with new goals that now included debt reduction, solvency, keeping one home and so forth, we were able to begin to formulate a plan that included retirement for them both by the age of 68. They chose to sell all of their properties, including *both* of their luxury homes. They then purchased one lovely but smaller property with good land in a more rural setting, away from the spending temptations of their high-living city society life.

What they gained—more time together, a quieter life—actually allowed them to begin cross-breeding beautiful roses on their new property. It wasn't retirement, but, unexpectedly, they found that the choices they had now made for themselves were proving to be far better for their health and quality of life. They worked from a budget for the first time, and aggressively stayed on track in their goal to reduce debt. In their more modest but oddly more satisfying and gracious picture, they are on track to retire by age 68.

They credited the Seasons of Advice model for empowering them to make the proactive choices. "Seasons is the best thing that happened for us," Andrew said. "Otherwise, we were a ship without a chart on high seas; we didn't know where we were, or how bad things were." Maxine said she wished they'd come to us sooner, "but we're thrilled with how things have turned around, we love our new life. If we'd stayed on our other course, we wouldn't even have known what hit us when we went down!"

Angela and Walter

Another couple, Angela and Walter, are clients we've worked with for many years, and their story is quite a contrast to Maxine and Andrew's. One of the goals we worked toward over time was their dream of purchasing a second home in Georgia, where they both grew up, along the southern coast and as near the water as possible. That was their main goal, along with the goal to retire as soon as possible to enjoy that home. He's 62, she's 59. They have no children together, but Walter has children in their 20's from a previous marriage.

Over the years, we've helped them keep those goals in sight and facilitated a plan to fulfill them. Each year we would crunch the numbers, run projections, confirm assumptions, and build the reserve to purchase the second home. Because we were prepared, as the prices recently came down in the depressed coastal towns in which they were interested, we were ready to take advantage of an opportunity. Remember, one of the things one plans for is the ability to take rapid advantage of a good opportunity.

When we did Goal Tracking with them, we were able to identify the fact that we could now accelerate their plan. We confirmed it with a look at the cash flow and taxes. We allocated the appropriate assets, they went house shopping, soon made an offer, and it was accepted. They were able to make this exciting purchase years ahead of schedule. Even better, they were able to get much more house and be closer to the water because of opportunities in the depressed market. They were thrilled their dream-come-true was even better than how they had dreamed it. They were still on track to retire as planned as well. In two years Angela would retire and move to this new home and Walter would join her on weekends until he retires in four years from his thriving professional supplies business. That was the plan—six months ago.

Remember that life always offers us surprises. Unexpectedly, Walter's business partner offered him a buyout. So he and Angela began to take a look at what they would need to make sure they could still support their cash flow needs. We looked in close detail at their actual spending and projections. We identified what the dollar amount would be. We looked at their assorted investments and identified some to liquidate.

In the end, Walter was able to discuss with his partner a reasonable retirement package, which they agreed upon. This meant that Angela and Walter could retire together three years earlier. They now have clear plans for their retirement that include pursuits of great interest to both of them, and they are delighted to get started on this new journey so far ahead of schedule.

Angela and Walter and Andrew and Maxine had similar incomes but very different dreams, with very different money styles. Angela and Walter had dreams that were ambitious yet grounded in good planning. They were always aware of where they were relative to their goals. In contrast, Andrew and Maxine were unrealistic in their dreams, unwise in their lifestyle, and disconnected from their goals. Without a roadmap, there was no way they could complete their journey. We helped them create that roadmap, and now both couples will retire with a lovely home and time to spend together in ways they desire.

Both couples have the investments, insurances and especially the peace of mind they need to carry them through any difficulties that may arise so that they can remain financially secure to the end of their days. One couple got to do this ten years ahead of the other, entirely free of debt, and with a more generous retirement income. However, goal setting, tracking and planning did save the day for Andrew and Maxine, pulling them back from the brink of a serious crisis and a very uncertain future. As they now grow award-winning roses in their free time and enjoy one another more, they also have excellent health, and are on track to be debt free in three more years, after which they will be able to retire as planned.

These couples demonstrate a process that illuminates retirement thinking and planning. The process will work for you too, just as it did for another client named Bob. Bob is a single man who told us from the beginning that he would never retire because he loved his work. That didn't mean he didn't have goals for the later stage of his life. "I want to be prepared for surprises if I can't work, or if I or my parents have unmanageable expenses. I just want to be ready," he told us. "I also want to be able to give my two nephews a modest nest egg to help them get started, and I want to leave a charitable endowment as my legacy."

Whether you plan to stop work or not, everyone has dreams and plans for the last third of his or her life, and these dreams always include both security and more freedom of choice. So is *your* retirement a reality or a mirage? The answer is that it can be whatever you want it to be, if you follow the logical progression set forth in this book.

Some people are extravagant; others are thrifty. Some are impulsive and unwise, wanting to spend ten cents of every dime in their pocket. While Seasons is not a "money rehab" system, the Seasons method can assist anyone who is willing to work from it, whether individually, as a couple, or as a family. The system is calibrated to help you envision, plan, understand, make decisions, control or direct spending as needed, and stay on track with your best goals.

There is certainly no more satisfying work, in our opinion, than helping clients plan for retirement in a way that becomes a reality, not an ever-flickering mirage on the horizon.

As for us...are you serious? We have no plans to retire, ever. We're having far too much fun!

A Retirement Self Quiz

So how much *do* you need to retire? Do your expected requirements meet or exceed your projected resources at retirement? What is your financial independence status? Here is a suggested rule of thumb.

First calculate your requirements. If you want to be conservative in your investments, multiply your estimated annual spending before income taxes by 25 and compare that number to your available resources.

Watch out for expenses that will end or adjust, such as mortgages that will pay down or education costs that will not exist in the future.

Now calculate your projected available resources. Add up all your after-tax investment assets, plus two-thirds of your before-tax assets such as IRAs 401(k)s etc.

If your available resources meet or exceed your requirements, that's a really good sign. You should be good to go. But what if it's not?

You could consider raising your allowable risk, which, as we defined in the Asset Allocation chapter means living with more volatility and a lower level of probability. If you were to move from conservative with little or no volatility to let's say moderate, you can lower the multiple from 25 to 18. This will help a lot.

If you still have the need, and the stomach for it, you could consider an aggressive portfolio, which could lower the multiple to 13 or almost one-half the amount you needed as a conservative investor.

This guidance is not a substitute for expert financial planning but can give you an idea where you stand.

"*Only as you do know yourself can your brain serve you as a sharp and efficient tool. Know your own failings, passions and prejudices so you can separate them from what you see.*"

BERNARD BARUCH, financier (1870-1965)

"*The thing that is really hard, and really amazing, is giving up on being perfect and beginning to work on becoming yourself.*"

ANNA QUINDLEN, journalist (1952–)

Chapter 9

Your Investment Personality

ARE YOU DRIVEN, AMIABLE,
EXPRESSIVE OR ANALYTIC?

W E HUMANS ARE capable of a wide range of behaviors under various circumstances. The infamous Three D's (Death, Divorce and Disaster) are extreme stressors that can cause us to act uncharacteristically. That said, there are certain social or personality types that respond in fairly predictable ways, whether to routine challenges or sudden unusual events or life changes that can and do crop up in all our lives from time to time.

Since this book focuses on how you feel about money, we try to also look at instincts which play a role in sound decision making. How we address our financial decisions is many times dictated by our essential personality types, which have been labeled in numerous ways by different experts. Some of these experts are psychologists or psychiatrists; some of them behaviorists, marketing professionals, sociologists and anthropologists. At the end of this chapter we have included a table that shows the ways in which several of these experts have labeled different social styles. We have also included a few charts that will allow you to get a sense of your own personal characteristics.

In this book, we are offering you four classically accepted personality types (also called social types) in a somewhat different context: we use these distinctions to help you understand how different types of people (yourself included) think, feel, act and react when it comes to financial matters. For our purposes, we are using these differences to assess how people differ in their risk tolerance and how they may be expected to react when things go wrong.

The four social style models we have utilized here have been adapted from the Merrill and Reid model of social behavior. Their charts are reprinted with permission from David W. Merrill and Roger H. Reid, bestselling co-authors of *Personal Styles & Effective Performance*. Renowned marketers, the Merrill and Reid four-quadrant personality assessments were designed to help business executives understand their people. The intention was to help individuals and teams work at peak performance, separately and together. When you know why you feel and react the way you do—what presses your buttons—you are in a much better position to make your personal social style work for you in the money realm as well as in other areas of life.

The four personality types brilliantly described in great detail by Merrill and Reid are Driver (Aggressive-Intellectual), Amiable (Passive-Emotional), Expressive (Aggressive-Emotional) and Analytical (Passive-Intellectual).

All this also adds up to what kinds of investors they are, which makes understanding each person's attitudes and concerns especially important to us for the kind of work we do. These distinctions allow us to honor the lens through which our clients (and we!) look at the world. The end game for us is our ability to effectively help them balance their portfolios and invest their money in the way that keeps them both financially secure and comfortable with their choices.

Understanding who you are in the matter of investments should be important to you too. Being able to recognize which of these four personalities best describes you allows you to see your reactions for what they are and make any necessary adjustments. In certain circumstances, understanding why you react as you do and being able to tempter or control those automatic reactions may be the key to your successfully weathering changes in the marketplace as well as in your life circumstances.

One caveat we think is critically important to point out: There is no good or bad, right or wrong style. These types are an explanation, not an excuse or judgment.

Identifying personality types

One way researchers determine the style of others is to listen to what they talk about, their tone of voice, how fast or slow they speak. They also look at their body language, responsiveness, and how well they listen. Keep in mind that once you determine which of the four quadrants you mainly fall into, three-quarters of the people you interact with in life are different from you.

If you listen carefully, you can hear significant differences in how people communicate. Drivers tend to say "I will." Expressives tend to say "I want." Analytics tend to say "I think." Amiables generally say, "I feel." Drivers talk very, very fast, while Expressives talk fast but less rapidly. Analytics talk at moderate speed and Amiables speak slower. Drivers make intense eye contact, lean forward and may keep their facial expressions neutral. Expressives are similar but also make lots of gestures and exhibit controlled facial expressions. Analytics lean back, keep their expressions neutral, and use fewer gestures. Amiables lean back, make good eye contact, and make normal gestures.

Drivers get right to the point and can be outspoken, even formal. Expressives are more informal, even casual, animated and excitable. Analytics can seem unresponsive, but they are just being reserved and cautious. They may also appear preoccupied. Amiables are friendly, responsive and love conversation. Drivers can be poor listeners, control the conversation and like to interrupt and summarize. ("Let's get to the point.") Expressives listen, react and talk a lot. Amiables are great listeners; they really care what you are saying but are slow to react.

Again, this is about how we express ourselves most of the time, not all the time. Many of us (your authors included) don't fit squarely in one group or another. However, we do each have one dominant personality style that we use day to day. Recognizing pros and cons of your specific personality style can help you understand how to better deal with your relationships to others as well as how your money is being invested, how your portfolio is balanced, and how you regard money overall. Now let us consider the characteristics of each type.

Driver

According to Merrill and Reid, Driver types are characterized by a more aggressive approach to dealing with business and an intellectual approach to their personal dealings. They tend to be fast-paced, results-oriented and to-the-point kind of people. This is how they describe the behaviors of Drivers, along with the three other personality types.

Driver personality types tend to display the following characteristics:

- Assertive dress and body posture

- An "all business" sort of attitude

- A sense of impatience

- A desire to control the negotiation

- A predilection for an environment that is organized without being overly neat

Preferences: Driver types are interested in business first and social interaction later. They view their time as valuable and will be put-off by a lengthy presentation. Get to the point of the presentation without getting bogged down in extraneous details; focus primarily on the specific methods to solve their problems and improve their business. Driver type personalities will be less interested in how sociable and friendly you are, and more interested in seeing demonstrable proof of your competence. Because this type of person is quick to reach a decision, it is imperative that you make a good first impression, and that your initial presentation is strong and confident.

The following activities and approaches are not well suited to this personality type:

- A "chatty," informal approach to the presentation: This type of personality is looking for a professional, not a buddy.

- Too much detail: Driver personalities are interested in the bottom line; focus on the tangible gains they will see from your service, not on the nuts and bolts details. If they want additional information concerning the process, they will ask for it.

- Soft approach: Driver types will be much more responsive to an aggressive, assertive style. A softer style may make them doubt the speaker's confidence and ability to deliver.

Amiable

Amiable types are characterized by a more passive approach to dealing with business and an emotional approach to their personal dealings. They are friendly, eager-to-please and slow to make decisions.

Amiable personality types tend to display the following characteristics:

- Casual dress

- Friendly, positive attitude

- Hesitant about change

- Avoid conflict

- Uncomfortable with pressure

Amiable personalities are slow to decide, and may frequently change their minds. They demonstrate high buyer's remorse. With this person, it is important to be sympathetic and friendly. Amiable personalities seek approval and validation. Their decision making requires support and confidence. Most Amiables are people-oriented. Shared stories and anecdotes are welcome to illustrate information and decisions. Focusing less on the bottom line and more on how to relieve stress provides them with peace of mind.

The following activities and approaches are not well suited to this personality type:

- An overly aggressive approach: Amiable personalities dislike high-pressure situations; a hard approach will make them feel uncomfortable and threatened. If they feel threatened, they are unlikely to collaborate with you.

- Overly formal presentation: This type wants a more personal, friendly relationship with their professionals.

- Too "hands off": Unlike Analytical types, who prefer to be left alone to consider the decision, Amiable types prefer guidance and follow-up in order to be comfortable with their decisions. Follow up consistently without seeming aggressive or pushy.

Expressive

Expressive types are characterized by a more aggressive approach to dealing with business and an emotive approach to their personal dealings. They are energetic, impulsive and more interested in the big picture than they are in the details.

Expressive personality types tend to display the following characteristics:

- Assertive, flashy or flamboyant dress and mannerisms

- A tendency toward disorganization or messiness

- A desire to dominate the conversation (and perhaps to discuss non-business related issues)

- A sense of self-importance or pride

- Disinterested in details

Expressive types are fast-paced and excitable. They will be most likely to respond to someone who is obviously emotionally involved and who seems excited and animated. This type of personality thrives on recognition. It is not necessary (or desirable) to be overly effusive or ingratiating, but one or two sincere comments about their business will help make an Expressive personality more comfortable and receptive.

This type of personality tends to dislike details. When absorbing information, they prefer to focus on key points rather than on explaining the minutiae of the work. Use of anecdotes and stories help Expressives to absorb information. They may tend to get bored more easily.

The following activities and approaches are not well suited to this personality type:

- A dry, overly formal tone: Expressive personalities are not "all business," and will be put off by someone who is.

- Too much focus on detail: Remember that this type of personality is not particularly detail-oriented. A careful, step-by-step analysis of each point is likely to bore them. Expressives dislike deviating from the core concepts.

- Expressive personalities crave excitement, and are unlikely to be convinced by a "soft-sell."

Analytical

Analytical types are characterized by a more passive approach to dealing with business and an intellectual approach to their personal dealings. They are slower-paced, detail-oriented and analytical.

Analytical personality types tend to display the following characteristics:

- Conservative or formal dress

- Restrained mannerisms and calm demeanor

- Highly organized work space

- Very time-conscious

- Tend to be early for appointments

Analytical personalities are detail-oriented, careful and conservative in their business practices. They are unlikely to make snap decisions, and if they are fully convinced of your credibility and competence, they will be willing to accept new ideas and suggestions. This personality type will respond well to a careful, well thought out presentation that proceeds in a logical, point-by-point manner. They will want to know all the details of the issues, options and solutions.

Because Analytical types are extremely detail-oriented, they tend to take their time making decisions. Effective follow-up procedures are of critical importance. Others may use "I need some time to consider it" as a put-off; when an Analytical personality says they need to think about it, they are probably being sincere.

The following activities and approaches are not well suited to this personality type:

- A high-energy, "pushy" approach: Analytical types are methodical and will prefer to take their time reaching a decision.

- A pressuring approach is likely to irritate them or make them uncomfortable with you.

- An informal or overly casual presentation: To build credibility with this type, it's best to be all-business.

- Too little detail: Do not attempt to gloss over details. Unlike the other personality types, Analytical personalities are genuinely interested in a high level of detail. A lack of detail maybe interpreted as a lack of knowledge, or (even worse) that someone is deliberately hiding something.

- Seeing the world through different lenses

As we said earlier, there are many different systems of categorizing personalities, and the specific system used is less important than having a general understanding of the differences in style that come into play.

When any of us are able to quickly identify our own and other people's personality types, we will know the "how's" and "why's" of what to say to meet their needs and our own. This helps with financial decision making, especially when trying to coordinate with someone else. Speaking the same "language" helps us feel truly understood. Feeling understood and respected for who you are and how you view things creates a connectivity that makes us able to work together for a common goal—in this case, your financial security—in the most powerful and effective way.

To successfully communicate with others, we need to recognize and appreciate our differences. This allows us to communicate in the most effective way with others. Focusing on the desired outcome to the point of ignoring these differences can make you ineffective. For example, get emotional with an Analytical when he or she wants "the plain facts" and you lose their trust. They will tune you out. Throw cold numbers at an Expressive or Amiable and they will likewise tune you out. Expect the Driver type to be assertive since they are control-taking and decisive personalities, then you won't be put off by their attitudes or behaviors.

Here are more descriptions of these four types from Merrill and Reid:

Analytical – Analytical people are systematic, well organized and deliberate. These individuals appreciate facts and information presented in a logical manner as documentation of truth. They enjoy organization and completion of detailed tasks. Others may see him or her at times as being too cautious, overly structured, someone who does things too much "by the book."

- controlled
- orderly
- precise
- disciplined
- deliberate
- cautious
- diplomatic
- systematic
- logical
- conventional

Driver – They thrive on the thrill of the challenge and the internal motivation to succeed. Drivers are practical folks who focus on getting results. They can do a lot in a very short time. They usually talk fast, direct and to the point. They are often viewed as decisive, direct and pragmatic.

- action-orientated
- decisive
- problem solver
- direct
- assertive
- demanding
- risk taker
- forceful
- competitive
- independent
- determined
- results-orientated

Amiable – They are dependable, loyal and easygoing. They like things that are nonthreatening and friendly. They hate dealing with impersonal details and cold hard facts. They are usually quick to reach a decision. An Amiable is often described as a warm person and sensitive to the feelings of others but sometimes wishy-washy.

- patient
- loyal
- sympathetic
- team person
- relaxed
- mature
- supportive

- stable
- considerate
- empathetic
- persevering
- trusting
- congenial

Expressive – Very outgoing and enthusiastic, with a high energy level. They are also great idea generators, but usually do not have the ability to see the idea through to completion. They enjoy helping others and are particularly fond of socializing. They are usually slow to reach a decision. They are often thought of as talkative, overly dramatic, impulsive and manipulative.

- verbal
- motivating
- enthusiastic
- convincing
- impulsive
- influential
- charming
- confident
- dramatic
- optimistic
- animated

The Wilson Learning Corporation went farther with the four Social Style distinctions created by Merrill and Reid. While using the four main leadership styles—Analytical, Driver, Amiable, and Expressive—the people at Wilson Learning Corporation further broke these down into four social behavior styles they labeled EMOTE, CONTROL, ASK, TELL.

All this information will not only inform your interaction with others but will also help you interpret your instincts. This is important in helping you to make sound financial decisions.

"*Getting your house in order and reducing the confusion gives you more control over your life. Personal organization somehow releases or frees you to operate more effectively.*"

LARRY KING, TV personality (1933–)

"*Science is organized knowledge. Wisdom is organized life.*"

IMMANUEL KANT, philosopher (1724–1804)

Chapter 10

Getting Out From Under the Paperwork

WHAT YOU CAN SAFELY DISCARD

E VERY CERTIFIED PUBLIC Accountant on earth has a story (or several stories) about clients who came in for a meeting on taxes with the proverbial cardboard box, shoebox, briefcase, or even large black plastic lawn bag filled with every manner of receipts and other assorted pieces of paper, and proceeded to dump it all on his desk or conference table. The Certified Financial Planner® is certainly not immune. This happens to CPAs, CFPs and related professionals more often than you might think.

> *"Here you go.*
> *These are my receipts for the past year.*
> *I'm sure you can sort it out."*

Another common situation many of us in financial services encounter is the client who tells us that their desks, tables, file drawers and even storage lockers are filled with papers of all sorts, and they simply have no idea what to keep and what they can safely discard. How many years of tax papers *does* one legally need to hang on to? There seems to be contradictory advice here, so people often store many more years than necessary of tax returns and receipts, tax deduction slips, client payment and employment records, real estate transaction records, marriage and divorce papers, and whatever else people hold on to for fear that they may need it "someday." This may not be as dire as hoarding, but for some people their papers are out of control, a source of great angst, and if they're not using up valuable office or home space unnecessarily, they're letting the papers gather dust under their beds or wastefully paying for a storage unit.

Just recently, one of our clients said that knowing what to discard has changed his life, and that this knowledge was for him one of the most valuable aspects of the Seasons of Advice approach. Now, for the first time in years, his desk is clean and neat, his drawers and files uncluttered and, best of all, he said, his *mind* feels far less cluttered!

You may find this topic somewhat mundane for a book focusing on sound financial decisions, but we promised you the good, bad and ugly. For some, this is the ugly. To fix a problem, you first have to understand it. From our own experience and talking to countless other financial advisors, tax accountants and other professionals who repeatedly have this experience, one fact is certain: a person's level of intelligence, professional success, social standing or prosperity has no bearing on who walks in with unsorted mountains of papers. However, whether that shoe box is literal or figurative (since they could also dump their papers and receipts out of one or more black garbage bags, cardboard boxes or suitcases) people do this kind of dumping for several reasons. One is convenience: it's a lot faster and easier to throw receipts and other potentially important papers into a pile for later sorting than to sit down and sort through it yourself on a daily or even weekly or monthly basis.

But the bigger reason, we began to understand, is that, as we said earlier, people are insecure about what to keep and what to discard, so they wind up keeping just about everything. We've had clients with twenty years' worth of tax papers, receipts, legal documents, including divorce papers—even, in one case, some angry exchanges in letters and e-mails from two earlier marriages. The list goes on, with some of the kept items patently absurd.

You don't have to be a hoarder to be buried in unnecessary papers. Misinformation, rumor, insecurity and good intentions can combine to fill bags and files and rooms with enough paper to circle the globe more than once. One client came in with five boxes from each of three (yes 3) marriages, as he explained, "in case any of it was needed." Another had 14 grocery bags with handles, each carefully labeled: gas receipts, sailing expenses, children's clothing, and so forth, including one that said "You never know." One woman brought in all of her aging mother's expense receipts and related papers because she wondered if she could claim them. We also had one couple whose husband insisted on coming in separately ahead of his wife because, as he put it, "She's going to drive me crazy with detailed questions about all this. I just want to know the bottom line."

In this case we actually met with the wife first, went into the detailed picture with her, and helped her understand what they needed to keep in future. It greatly relieved her tension level. Then we met with both to look at the whole picture. He got his bottom line, was happy as a clam—and so was she.

Rochelle was a client we began working with a few years ago. She had extreme anxiety about money in general and specifically which papers to keep. Her nervousness showed up as difficulty finishing sentences and a scattered manner. To our shock and surprise, all of this changed when we got her paperwork issues under control. We had also suggested she hire an organizer to help create a home filing and storage system, and that really worked for her. "I love order and detail," she told us. "Without it, I literally can't hear myself think!"

Although her case was extreme, many clients tell us that one of the most helpful things is to have certainty about what they really must keep and what they can discard. With a clear plan, they can create order out of the chaos. This combination of taking away what isn't part of their financial picture and organizing what is brings the real picture clearly into view. In fact, many clients report that this de-clutter and re-balance process allows them to see and understand their financial picture more realistically, and gives them a confidence in this arena they hadn't experienced before.

To relieve you of any possible "paper hoarding" proclivities of your own, we are sharing some of the information we use that has been extremely helpful in our practice.

Let's start with this suggestion: begin to consider an electronic scanner your new best friend. As they come in, you can put your recent bills and papers in a file, box or bag. Then, on a weekly or monthly basis, whether doing this yourself or paying someone the small amount it might cost to have them do it for you, scan everything into files on your computer—in the right categories, of course.

A blizzard of papers is much easier for everyone to deal with when it is electronic. An electronic blizzard doesn't accumulate in great drifts and piles, requiring "heavy machinery" to clear it, nor does it cause mind meltdown or brain freeze in the same way. It is also much easier for your tax people and other financial advisors to deal with.

The basic questions you need answered are: What should I keep? How long do I need to keep it? What do I need hard copy of and what can be electronic only? What should I shred or burn?

While there are many resources on the World Wide Web that provide this information, the best summary we have found to date was by a blogger named Madison DuPaix, owner and chief editor of www.mydollarplan.com. Madison started My Dollar Plan in 2007 as a way to share her passion for personal finance, including taxes, investing, retirement plans and seeking free money deals. When Madison isn't writing about personal finance, she's an enrolled agent who started a tax business on the side "just for fun" and is the founder of a local investment club. Before leaving corporate America behind to stay home with her three young children, Madison worked in the finance and insurance industry.

http://www.mydollarplan.com/
how-long-do-we-really-need-to-keep-those-papers/

How Long Do We Really Need to Keep Those Papers?
Posted by Madison DuPaix

As part of my effort to organize myself for the New Year, I've found that I'm starting to become a pack rat with papers.

While I was busy purging paper and backing up the electronic data, I realized that when we don't know how long to keep something, we end up keeping it forever... or not at all. Here's how long we should be keeping those important papers:

Forever

- Birth Certificates

- Marriage Certificates

- Divorce Certificates

- Death Certificates

- Military Documents

- Immunization Record

- Employment Records (Why)

- IRA Contributions

- Social Security Card

- Tax Returns: The IRS can audit your returns from 3 years ago; 6 years if you grossly under reported; indefinitely if you filed a fraudulent return or did not file. So you could pitch your returns after 7 years…however, if they claim you didn't file, and you pitched it… well, now you know why I put tax returns on the indefinite list! You can also request copies or transcripts of past tax returns.

Keep During Ownership

- Car Titles and Service Records

- Receipts, Manuals and Warranty Information for Appliances

- Receipts for Major Purchases like Jewelry, Furniture and Computers

Ownership Plus 7 Years

Even after you sell investments or real estate, you'll still need to keep the gain or loss documentation for tax purposes.

- Stocks, Bonds and Investment Records

- Savings Certificates

- Home Improvement Documentation

- Real Estate Records

7 Years

Many of the following will contain information that supports tax returns. Therefore it's best to keep the following for seven years:

- Canceled Checks

- Credit Card Statements

- Old Bank Statements

- Retirement Plan Contributions

- Supporting Documentation for Tax Returns

Until Specified Date

- Annual Retirement Statements: Until retirement and funds are exhausted.

- Insurance Policies – Until property is sold, policy expires, and all claims are settled.

- Wills: Until replaced by a new one.

Throw Away

- Receipts not used for Warranties, Taxes or Insurance

- Paycheck Stubs: Once you get your W-2, you can toss them

- Phone Bills not needed for taxes

- ATM Receipts

- Grocery Receipts

Now that your desk is all cleared off, let's move on to the last chapter, and see precisely how the accumulated Seasons of Advice strategies we've given you through this book can impact your life, and who you might want to add to your financial team for You, Inc.

"*For it is mutual trust, even more than mutual interest that holds human associations together.*"

H.L. MENCKEN, American journalist (1880–1956)

"*In almost every profession – whether it's law or journalism, finance or medicine or academia or running a small business – people rely on confidential communications to do their jobs. We count on the space of trust that confidentiality provides. When someone breaches that trust, we are all worse off for it.*"

HILLARY CLINTON, Secretary of State (1947–)

Chapter 11

The Realities of Working with a Financial Advisor

F INANCIALLY SECURE FOREVER: The Seasons of Advice® Solution offers a new way of thinking about your finances to help you make the right decisions at the right times. *Seasons of Advice* can become a valuable resource for you as a foundation for the organization of multiple financial tracks of information and priorities. While you need to be the helmsperson, your optimal success also depends on your ability to build an excellent team of professionals, such as your investment and tax advisors, and effectively manage them over time. You may have the time, interest and expertise to do this yourself, or you may choose to engage someone to help manage this process. This would mean that you delegate the strategic planning, implementation and coordination of your financial plan to a qualified professional. As you consider this option, let's consider the things you will want to be aware of and take into consideration.

1. Be clear about what you are looking for— what kind of advisor you want

The most common reason for an unsatisfactory outcome is a mismatch between what you expect and what the advisor delivers. There are many types of advisors imparting a wide spectrum of advice. Do you need a comprehensive professional or a specialist in one main area? Do you simply need a one-time analysis or would you benefit from an ongoing relationship? The reality is that it's your job to match your needs and expectations to the right kind of advisor. It's the advisor's role to accurately communicate their ability to deliver on your needs.

By now, having read through the book, you should have a good idea of the goals of your own financial plan. Reflecting on the type of expert you need, keep in mind any unique circumstances you have that may create the need for a professional with unique skills. This could include families with special needs, same sex relationships, geographic challenges, health issues, etc. It also could mean the need to deal with executive compensation programs, trusts and estates.

Naturally, it's best to put your goals on paper before you meet the advisor for the first time. Consider short-term and long-term goals separately. List any financial concerns you have. Finally, if you have a history of dealing with financial advisors, good or bad, it is beneficial to tell the prospective advisor what happened. Let them learn what makes you tick and understand the things they will need to do meet your expectations.

If the plan affects others such as a spouse, perhaps you should have a sit-down with them first. Should you and yours disagree on goals, risk tolerance, etc., make both points of view known to the advisor. A seasoned professional knows how to create a balance to serve varying styles and concerns.

Make sure you include concerns such as potential difficulties or possible detours or roadblocks. What happens if someone loses his or her job or becomes sick or disabled? As we saw in Chapter Six, there is a lot to plan for. Is this advisor strong in the important areas, or just an investment jockey?

If you choose to do your own planning, becoming, in effect, your own general contractor, you can hire specialists such as stockbrokers, insurance agents or mutual fund companies to do your bidding. There is also no shortage of well-intentioned relatives, co-workers, and financial hobbyists who would gladly give you free advice. However, no one, not even close family members, will ever know you in the same way that an excellent and caring personal financial advisor will. It's important to develop a trusting relationship. This becomes more and more critical as the stakes get larger and your goals closer.

2. Understand who you're dealing with and how everyone gets paid

Now is probably a good time to mention that the authors have achieved success primarily from an advice platform based on an affordable fee-based structuring versus transaction or percentage based systems. While this is successful for us, we do not suggest that this is the only platform to consider. When interviewing a potential financial advisor, try to do some advance homework. Check out a planner's website and social media page. Linked-In® may have the most relevant information, but posts on Facebook can be interesting and give you other insights.

Be clear what Broker/Dealer firm this individual is associated with. While it might not be immediately obvious, the Financial Industry Regulatory Authority (FINRA) requires that all financial advisors who deal with investments, insurance, etc. must be connected to a supervisory firm that is supposed to look out for you. This firm is known as the Broker/Dealer (BD) and you should know which firm the prospective advisor is connected to. You can learn more at **www.brokerdealerfirms.com/index. php**. This is important protection for you and can give you a valuable heads-up on what type of service and products you can expect. Some BD's carry names that would be very familiar, while some do not. You should research the various BDs to get a sense of their priorities, target markets, strengths and business philosophy.

Once you've met with the advisor, it's appropriate to request a copy of their *Form ADV Parts 1 and 2* disclosures, which they should be willing to provide on the spot. This document is intended to disclose all things legal and formal that you should know about the advisor and their Broker/ Dealer.

We recommend you only deal with advisors that have passed basic licensing requirements, as prescribed by regulatory agencies, to work in the financial advice business. As a bare minimum, confirm that any prospective advisor is currently licensed by FINRA if in the Unites States. This is known as the Series 7 license. You should also check the government's FINRA BrokerCheck® site at **www.brokercheck.finra.org** where you can learn more about the background and complaint history of the investment professional or firm. FINRA BrokerCheck provides an online database of information about brokers and brokerage firms as well as investment adviser firms and representatives. You can find out, among other things, whether your broker or investment adviser representative is licensed in your state to conduct business, and whether he or she has ever been sanctioned by securities regulators for violations of investment-related regulation or statute. While this should be your first stop for information, you should also consider consulting your state securities regulator, local consumer and investment groups or others who have established business relationships with a particular broker or investment adviser representative.

There are various professional designations advisors can work to achieve. The premier professional accreditation is the CFP® or Certified Financial Planner® designation. Those that have achieved CFP® designation have made the commitment you want to see in a prospective advisor. CPAs have a similar designation, Personal Financial Specialist (PFS) for those accountants who have demonstrated a commitment to providing personal financial planning advisory.

The Securities and Exchange Commission has an excellent Q&A on what you need to know before choosing an advisor. You can access this at www.sec.gov/investor/pubs/invadvisers. htm. It makes the important point that while most financial planners are investment advisers, *not every investment advisor is a financial planner.*

There are primarily two categories of work for which advisors are compensated, Financial Advice and Investment Advice. Be extremely clear on what you are being asked to pay for, when you are expected to pay it, what you will receive, when you will receive it, and how the information you receive should be used.

The majority of reputable advisors make a distinction between costs that cover Planning and Advice fee, and costs to Implement the Plan. The latter could cover research, trading and commissions, transaction fees, etc., which are commonly referred to as Asset Management Fees. When quoted a fee, don't hesitate to ask which one of these buckets that fee falls into. In some cases, advisors combine these into one fee for convenience. This combination, however, rarely saves you money and is sometimes controversial. You decide what's best for you. Ask for the advisor's *Fee Schedule*. In accordance with regulations, advisors must be consistent in what they charge their clients for the work performed. This can vary substantially across advisors. Make sure you ask!

When you hire a financial professional, you are expecting someone to bring targeted experience, process management as well as good judgment. Test your decision by asking yourself if this person is bringing unique skills you cannot or prefer not to provide for yourself. That, plus the knowledge that you are leveraging your precious time, is what is known as the value proposition.

Always discuss the methods of communication available to you. Will there be regular face-to-face meetings or primarily a telephone relationship? Perhaps you want to explore web teleconferencing where you can meet live over the Internet, an efficient method that is becoming popular. Ask the advisor if this option is available as it is an excellent way to manage your limited time.

Finally, ask if you are compelled to implement the advice strategies with this advisor, or can you implement separately or through someone else. There is no right or wrong answers here, but understand that if the advisor is not expecting any implementation income from your relationship, they may charge you a bit higher advice fee. This makes sense, but you need to be clear about these things from the start.

Professional financial advisors, the good ones, the real ones, do spend a large part of their income on the support infrastructure needed to deliver accurate and timely advice. Software is expensive. Staff is expensive. Rent is expensive. Even the cost to maintain licenses with continuing education requirements is becoming more and more expensive. There are lots of expenses! You need an advisor that invests continually in their business by staying current.

Ask the advisor how much time, on average, their practice spends on behalf of each client over the course of the year. Whatever fee you are quoted, understand what level of ongoing support will be dedicated to you. Ask about your advisor's support team, their backgrounds and responsibilities, and how they will be working for you in the long run. Your fee will be paying for their time as well. Keep in mind that the advisor is also paying the B/D for support services such as compliance oversight, insurance, marketing costs, technology.

If the quoted fee seems too low, this should be a red flag that you may incur hidden fees down the road.

Some firms rely on selling you investments from their inventory. When this occurs, they may be receiving an additional markup on the products, which increases your costs. Occasionally, an investment may be good enough to warrant it, but again you should know what you are paying for from the start.

With regard to investment fees, it has become more common today to be quoted an overall asset management "wrap" fee. This can come with or without trading costs added to the base fee. Again, we are not passing judgment but you need to be clear what is included and what is not.

Overall, though, expect to pay somewhere between 1-2% of the assets under management for investment fees. Is this a good deal? Is it too much? Our suggestion on how to answer this question is this: If the fees are going for good things like research, active management, etc. and the net return after these fees exceed the indices they are measured against, you are getting value and that should be your goal. Low fees do not necessarily mean you will make the most money. Quality asset managers usually will outperform the indices even though you might pay more to work with them.

Ask your prospective advisor to show you a list of some of the investments they regularly use. You're looking for diversification across all asset classes. It will be more costly to spread your money around by apportioning it to several different money managers, but concentrating your assets too much can also cause problems. Your financial advisors can go over the benefits of diversifying across multiple managers versus concentrating on one or a few.

Ask about breakpoints available which encourage you to concentrate more money with the same money manager. While this has its cost benefits, it may not assure you that you have the best investments over time. The financial advisor will help you understand if this is best or whether it's best to diversify. You will probably be better off if you work with a financial advisor who can bring a wide variety of investment choices to you. Within the industry, this is mostly known as having an "open architecture."

To insure more successful investing, have a structured process to update older investments with new and more effective ones. Don't get caught up in the day's hot stocks. The key is to keep things fresh. The long term investment challenge is most definitely achieved through the proactive process your advisor uses to determine the right time to replace your holdings with something better. You need to understand their process and philosophy, and keep in mind that success should not be just measured on trading gains but ultimately on whether you can achieve the goals you set for yourself and your family.

Should you negotiate fees? You can try, and might be successful, but in our opinion it may not be in your best interest to ask the advisor to cut corners. This could lead to an inconsistent long-term experience that will not really help you. It's not uncommon to hear among advisors that their family and friends usually get the worst service. It's not because we don't love them but we usually fail to charge them properly, if at all, and that keeps them out of the system. Ultimately, if you believe the fees are too high, most definitely shop around instead of trying to negotiate.

3. It's a match! Finding the right advisor

In evaluating a potential financial advisor, your family's future CFO, financial planner and protector, it's important to choose someone you feel you can develop a good rapport with. It's likely the advisor may someday have to interact with everyone in the family, so assess the personality traits you think might fit best.

Receiving a referral from others in a similar situation who are dealing with similar issues and challenges is a preferred way to begin your search. Obviously, those who have seen their advisor perform in good and bad markets, and in crisis situations as well as in times of prosperity, are a great referral source.

Accountants may also be a good referral source for you. Keep in mind that the accountant sees a narrow slice of the financial advisor's work, mostly on the investment side. Nonetheless, they can steer you to people who have dealt with tax issues thoughtfully and proactively. The Board of Standards of CFPs has a Web site (**www.CFP.net**) you can visit to get a referral as does the AICPA's CPA/PFS at **www.AICPA.org**.

You won't have a problem getting recommendations. The trick is to listen for things that make a difference. To have someone referred to you because they are "really nice" or "responsive when I call" is not enough. Have the referrer describe their process, the frequency and quality of contact, and even the software they use. Also, you really won't know if this is the right person unless your referring friend has at least two years' experience with this advisor or knows others that have and are happy with that advisor.

Many financial advisors have had previous careers, perhaps in a financially related occupation or perhaps something very different. As we've mentioned, this is a relatively young industry. Their previous professional occupations can serve you well. For instance, if they were teachers, they may have good communication skills and a good ability to explain concepts.

Regardless of the reasons you choose the advisor, you are well served to heed the Old Russian proverb to "trust, but verify."

4. Try to stay out of the news

Unfortunately, it's not hard to find stories of individuals who have been taken advantage of by unscrupulous financial professionals. While it may astonish us that people allow themselves to be put in that position, the truth is that we are all vulnerable to such dangerous predators. It's that greed vs. need thing we discuss in the book. If you want to stay "Financially SECURE Forever" you will need to avoid the pitfalls you may encounter. What follows is by no means an exhaustive list of do's and don'ts. You can research these more on the Internet. However, here are some of our favorites which when heeded might serve to protect you from becoming involved in a bad situation.

Cash transactions

This should be common sense, but NEVER give cash, actual *cash paper money*, to an advisor for investments. And certainly never receive cash payments from the advisor for any reason whatsoever. You could inadvertently become involved in a money-laundering scheme, or worse. No cash!

Neither a borrower nor a lender be

Shakespeare's Polonius counseled his son using this now famous aphorism. You would be well served to heed this same advice when it comes to your financial advisor. It's just not a good idea. Don't do it. The advisor knows it is expressly prohibited and it is unethical. Related to this no-borrow-no-lend dictum, let us also caution you against entering into a business relationship with your advisor.

Selling unapproved products

The Broker/Dealer shares in the responsibility of making sure investment products sold by their representatives have undergone a fair amount of due diligence. That is not to say that all investments are good investments, or that a loss is not possible, but there are basic protections in place when the Broker/Dealer has approved the recommended investments.

Make sure all investments you make through your financial advisor appear on the monthly statement and not on a side document. As we mentioned before, ask to receive statements directly from the Broker/Dealer, not from the advisor.

Watch out for unsuitable investments

Discovering that the advisor sells the same products to both younger and older clients alike may be a flag that the advisor does not properly consider age. We have seen portfolios of 80-year-olds in low tax brackets that would be more appropriate for people with a longer timeframe (i.e. younger) who pay taxes at a higher rate. If you have short-term goals, it is unwise to pair them up with long-term investments such as stocks.

We have all read stories about how some rogue financial advisors had steered their clients to investments that bore much greater risk than their clients understood. Stay in your comfort zone by reviewing your investments no less than semi-annually. And stay aligned with your goals.

Buying investments with no marketable quotes

There are exceptions to this but most investments should be marketable. You should be able to find quotes on the exchanges, or elsewhere, without relying solely on the advisor. There are many reasons you may choose an investment not readily marketable; that is fine if you clearly understand the nature of these investments and their limitations. That means you must put in the time to understand what you are investing in. If you don't have the time or comfort, stay away from investments not easily resold (i.e. not marketable).

Avoid discretionary relationships until you are comfortable with an advisor

Some types of investments, mutual funds and investment trusts for instance, allow a portfolio manager to decide what to buy or sell and what to pay for these investments without your permission. These are institutional-based investments that are widely used, highly regulated, well examined and considered a safe way to go.

Differing from these are *personal* investment accounts that give the broker or money manager the right to trade the components of such accounts virtually in any way they want and without approval from the client. These are called "discretionary trading accounts" and need additional attention from you to make sure all is working well. You also need to understand how these accounts may put you in greater risk. There are many appropriate uses for a discretionary account, but tread carefully. First, do not even consider this type of arrangement if you are not familiar with the manager or find they are not well supervised. If you feel unfamiliar with investments or are hesitant by nature, its best to avoid this type of relationship. If you do decide to allow your assets to be traded on a discretionary basis, please do not put all your money with that manager, even if they have a really good track record. Weigh the benefits and risks thoughtfully.

Examine your statements carefully

As basic as these sounds, one of the most important commitments you need to make to your own finances is to review your monthly statements. Even the most well-intentioned financial advisor relies on technology—which means "stuff happens." Don't assume your financial advisor actually even *sees* your statements. Internal reporting to the advisor is usually made from a different system. Discrepancies do exist. We suggest you schedule one session with your financial advisor to review your statement so that you know how it actually flows. You should carve out about a half hour each month to review it yourself.

While we're on the topic, beware of possibly fraudulent performance statements generated by the advisor. It's way too easy to simply generate a manual report. They are not necessarily inaccurate, but as we've said reports received directly from the Broker/Dealer are more reliable. The difference might be hard to detect, but understand that manually generated reports give you no protection and are a familiar element cited in many public fraud cases.

Above all, trust your instincts!

Try to choose an advisor or an advisory team that can grow with you over the decades. Undoubtedly, as you work together, a variety of annoying issues will arise, some more serious than others. There will be miscommunications, appointments cancelled, calls not returned and, more seriously, the occasional shortfall on investment returns. If you have chosen wisely and your instincts agree, keep these things in perspective. If you believe your advisor possesses an absolute commitment to protecting you and your family and dealing with the serious issues of longevity, inflation, health care and so forth, you might let some of these transgressions go. If you do not feel this way, or if the problems become chronic, move on!

The reality of working with a financial advisor is that it is a complicated and sometimes inexact business that requires flexibility and confidence from the clients to help advisors do their best.

As financial advisors ourselves, we do not take our roles lightly. Our clients entrust us with their most important dreams and concerns. So, yes, we get it and while they select us, rest assured that we select them as well. Each and every relationship is heartfelt. If it's the right fit, most will evolve on an emotional level and practical and productive level. That is precisely what makes this a great business as far as we're concerned!

Understanding Your Account Statement

According to the Securities Industry Association, here's a checklist for you to help you understand your account statement.

www.in.gov/sos/securities/files/UnderstandingYour
AccountStatement.pdf

1. Verify the activity in your account:
   - Identify the time period covered by the statement;
   - Find your beginning and ending balances;
   - Verify withdrawals and additions to your account;
   - Identify dividends and interest received in your account and understand the source (i.e., the specific security investment) of that income; and
   - Verify all transactions against trade confirmations.

2. **Confirm basic account data and compare it to previous statements:**

   - Check account numbers;

   - Verify that any address changes are reflected accurately; and

   - Compare the beginning balance of your current statement with the ending balance of the previous statement.

3. **Look for a summary of your holding:**

   - Identify security descriptions, dollar value, the quantity of shares of each investment, and maturity dates, if applicable; and

   - Make sure that the calculated portfolio percentages agree with your diversification and asset allocation objectives.

4. **Be sure that you understand performance data:**

   - Review your portfolio's gains and losses;

   - Determine which securities gained or lost value;

   - Assess whether the net value reflects an increase or decrease; and

   - Review whether portfolio gains and losses represent investment opportunities.

5. **If the account has multiple owners, make sure that all account owners have the opportunity to review the statement.**

6. **Review the margin activity and interest charges, if applicable.**

7. Call and ask questions if you are confused or if your investment situation has changed as to goals, risk tolerances, or timeframe.

8. Report any discrepancies promptly. It is extremely important to address any discrepancy quickly after you receive your account statement. Call your investment representative. If he or she is not available, ask for the branch manager.

"*Thinking well is wise; planning well, wiser; doing well wisest and best of all.*"

PERSIAN PROVERB

"*We now accept the fact that learning is a lifelong process of keeping abreast of change. And the most pressing task is to teach people how to learn.*"

PETER DRUCKER, business expert (1909–2005)

Staying Comfortable With Any Challenge Life Throws at You

"It was the best of times. It was the worst of times."

CHARLES DICKENS WROTE those opening words to his 1859 novel, *A Tale of Two Cities*, which was set in London and Paris before and during the French Revolution. The same could be said of our world today. Think about it for a moment; there is much to be thankful for, and much that we human beings need to do to make our world a safer, saner, happier place for each and every one of us sharing this planet, including those who will come after us.

In our arena, as we said at the outset, we seek to help those with a degree of accumulated wealth understand how to best secure their present and future, by working at the outset from a definite but fluid Wish List of how they want their lives to be, and how they want their accumulated assets to serve them and those they love.

In this book we have endeavored to offer ideas and information gained from our many years of experience doing just that. As the Seasons of Advice model began to develop as a powerful tool for our clients, it became our dream to share this in a way that might inspire people to utilize some of the principles and bring value to their personal financial worlds. These are the best of times in terms of advances in science, medicine and technology, and a bright future is opening in those areas. Financially speaking, it may not be exactly the worst of times, but it is a time of great shifts and change. There are many uncertainties. World financial markets are sometimes volatile, sometimes unstable and often vulnerable to unexpected influence from any quarter. More than ever, these are times that require wisdom, prudence and planning.

Think of the ubiquitous squirrel. That furry-tailed little creature we see everywhere, in towns and cities, parks and wooded areas, has an innate industrious soul built into its DNA. All summer, it stores nuts for the winter, so that it and its young will not starve when blankets of snow cover the ground. Likewise, we humans put aside savings, or buy property and other tangibles we hope will serve and protect our family and our dreams and goals.

An important difference is this: if the squirrel puts aside 500 nuts, when winter comes he has 500 nuts—no more, no less. For us it works a little differently. If we have a five hundred thousand dollar portfolio, it can grow. We can also lose some or all of it due to inflation, or to bad investments, changes in personal or professional circumstances, etc. Unlike the squirrel, we might unwisely or unwittingly use all our nuts in the first weeks of winter and face a difficult shortfall.

None of us want to be a squirrel that is struggling to hold on. We want the fruits of our labors, the funds we work hard for and sacrifice for, to likewise work for us.

Our intent is to live better, be more generous, perhaps enjoy a comfortable retirement sooner rather than later and hopefully also leave a financial nest egg for our children or other beneficiaries. We try our best to implement actions that will ensure that we can do so. We hope we have the right things in place to achieve it but we are not always clear about what is needed or certain we are prepared for the necessary contingencies in an uncertain world. We know that even the best laid plans can be suddenly vulnerable. How can we be sure our plan covers us? How can we best move through the many challenges life is likely to throw at us?

That is exactly why we created the Seasons of Advice® approach—to offer practical, workable, effective solutions that afford security in the face of what seemingly cannot be planned for are built into the Season's system. This includes:

Your Vision– and, continue to dream, to learn who you are and what you really need and want.

Set Goals – and use them as your North Star to navigate any waters from calm to volatile.

Assess and Reassess – Visit and revisit cash flow, taxes, insurance, investments, family, etc., each in its own Season, and each relative to and informing the other Seasons.

Clarify and organize – in each Season and build your life plan and portfolio on this continuing renewal of information. In this way, your picture continues to be one of your specific relationships to current factors in your life and in the world.

Communicate – share the right information, and your changing picture, with your team of experts so that they can serve you in the best way.

What makes the Seasons of Advice approach different from others is that it is designed to help you take everything into account: your personal style or type, your own unique dreams and needs, how the brain works in financial decision making, personal patterns that may not serve you, unexpected challenges and opportunities, the realities of your personal world and the many factors in the financial market. There is much to be considered and tracked. That's why we developed this approach.

We hope you enjoyed this book and that it has helped you better understand how you can stay comfortable with any challenge life throws at you and gain financial security forever. If you still have questions, please visit us at our website at www.FinanciallySecureForever.com. We would also be delighted to hear from you with any comment or feedback you care to share.

Respectfully,

Charles Hamowy
Christopher Conigliaro

About the Authors

Together and separately, Charles and Chris continue to bring their Seasons of Advice® program to many other certified financial planners, advisors, and others in their industry, educating them on the strategic skills and techniques they need to help their financially successful clients, individuals and families maintain and grow their wealth.

 **Charles Hamowy CPA, CFP®**
After graduating from New York University in 1978, Charles Hamowy began his career in the accounting profession as a Certified Public Accountant. After a successful decade-long career in accounting he redirected his passion to help others build their personal financial success, adding the Certified Financial Planner® credential to his professional designations. Charles is also an executive compensation planning specialist. In 1998, he joined forces with Christopher Conigliaro, CFP, to form a wealth advisory firm. A former financial radio show host and commentator, Charles is a sought after media expert and public speaker addressing topics from investment portfolio design to

planning for life's uncertainties. He takes great pride in having incubated several successful small startup businesses.

Born in Brooklyn, Charles Hamowy lives and works in New York City.

Christopher Conigliaro CFP®

After graduating from Hofstra University in 1993, Christopher Conigliaro went directly into the financial services industry, where he has happily remained for his entire career. A Certified Financial Planner, Chris manages the successful financial advisory practice in midtown New York City that he co-owns with Charles Hamowy. A dynamic speaker on the subject of personal wealth management strategies, he is also a popular media expert on a wide range of investment products. Christopher's research is in high demand and is utilized regularly by many industry professionals. He lives in New York State and, with Charles, works in the firm's offices in midtown Manhattan.

For more information, Charles and Christopher can be reached at **info@SeasonsofAdvice.com**